Partisans in an Uncertain World

Partisans in an Uncertain World: The Psychoanalysis of Engagement

Paul Hoggett

'an association in which the free development of each
is the condition of the free development of all'

Free Association Books / London / 1992

To Rose, for being who you are

First published in Great Britain in 1992 by
Free Association Books
26 Freegrove Road
London N7 9RQ

© Paul Hoggett 1992

The right of Paul Hoggett to be identified as the
author of this work has been asserted by him in
accordance with the Copyright, Designs and
Patents Act, 1988.

British Library Cataloguing in Publication Data
Hoggett, Paul
Partisans in an uncertain world: the psychoanalysis
of engagement.
1. Psychoanalysis
I. Title
150. 195

ISBN 1-85343-143-5
ISBN 1-85343-144-3 pbk

Typeset by Interpress Magazines (Pvt) Ltd, New Delhi, India
Printed and bound in Great Britain by
Billing and Sons Ltd, Worcester

Contents

Acknowledgements

I have learnt from many different people, each has taught me something different. The mid- and late 1970s were formative years for my own development, in terms of both my political and psychoanalytical understanding. Some of the people I met then remain in close contact with me, with others I have had conflicts and there have been separations; in other instances we have just drifted away.

First of all I would like to thank Ken Tarbuck. Ken taught me how to appreciate the depth and grandeur of the external world. A Marxist in the true sense, neither dogmatic nor academic, always struggling to understand, in a living and vivid way, how the present contains both our past and future. Hudson Pace showed me different things: an almost surreal sense of the everyday, a capacity to question the most obvious and disturb the most complacent. Finally, Sue Holland, who introduced me to psychoanalysis as a practical method of intervention, who taught primarily by allowing me to watch her work – speaking the unspeakable to individuals and families and thereby offering them the choice of relinquishing the pain they carried around with them.

I would also like to thank these three for going their own way, in a direction which brought few rewards. The privileges that I enjoy within a university are ones that they could have had if they had been prepared to compromise a little more. I thank them for not compromising.

There are others from this period I would like to mention: Marie Maguire, Jo Ryan and Julian Lousada, for being fellow travellers, good companions. I would also like to thank Barry Richards for enabling me to make the bridge between my South London days and my Bristol days, for drawing me into the circle around *Free Associations* in the early 1980s. And from this group I would particularly like to thank Bob Young, both for his consistent support and for the care he took in reading this manuscript. What Barry did for my engagement with psychoanalysis, Mike Davis did for my involvement in politics – he kept things alive, linkages going.

I would like to thank all of the people I have mentioned so far for another reason. They have all kept on going on, throughout the 1970s and throughout the 1980s; in Britain these have been two very contrasting decades. In different ways they have all kept on struggling to understand whilst keeping hold of an original vision, a vision that things could be different, that another way is always possible.

1

Introduction: The Political is Personal

As a child I once had a dream the theme of which has recurred in subsequent dreams of mine to this present day. The theme is simple – something terrible is happening to others, and I am the only witness. In the very first dream it concerned the children of my primary school. They had been laid out in rows at the Sheldon Road crossroads in Chippenham, a place I passed every day. The headmistress, Mrs Hooper, was inspecting their intestines. I remember her commenting that Clive Bane's were very clean. I looked upon this scene from behind a hedge. It didn't seem violent, just clinical.

Ever since then I have been suspicious of authority or, rather, of 'the authorities'. The point about the dream-scene is that its horror did not lie in what was being done to the bodies of my friends; there were no screams. Indeed, I had the sense that once the inspection was over their bodies would be sealed together again. No, the horror lay in the way in which the authorities had demonstrated their ability to do what they liked with us. It was a kind of rape, a violation of children. A few years ago, after some unrest in St Pauls, Bristol, the police rounded up, almost at random, dozens of people in the street. They were nearly all black. Back in the station many were made to strip, men and women, young and middle-aged, so that they could be searched for concealed weapons or drugs. They were also made to bend over, just in case they had something hidden inside their rectums. Of course, they've been practising strip-searches like this in Northern Ireland for fifteen years and more, mostly on women Republicans in places like Armargh prison.

1

These two examples, the one a dream, the other a real event, tell us something about terror: whilst it may be targeted upon the body, its real aim is to destroy the human spirit. For this reason terror is absolutely murderous even though, after it has had its way, our bodies may be left intact.

There is something about the world we live in today which is like this. For the forty years or so since the Second World War we have all lived in a world in which the authorities pretend to have kept the peace through a set of arrangements which, whilst they may have spared our bodies, have murdered our souls. In 1989, in Eastern and Central Europe, there were some signs of hope, of the reassertion of human value in a world of petrified spirits. One exception to this awakening within European nations is my own, Britain. Here we remained cowed, crushed by a regime which announced its ascendancy over a decade before through the words of St Francis of Assisi; a regime for which, at the time, no words could be found adequately to describe its meanness of spirit or callous indifference.

The thoughts and arguments which make up this book have their origins in the dying years of the last Labour Government. With hindsight it is now clear that what was passing was not just the Wilson–Callaghan era but more fundamentally a whole Labourist tradition which had reached down into the pores of British social democracy and the revolutionary Left alike. Many things could and have been said about the inadequacies of this tradition, and as to what will take its place all that can be said is that the future remains uncertain. In other essays and articles I have endeavoured with several associates to sketch the possibilities for a far more decentralized and democratic approach to the business of government and the organization of the Welfare State. Such a strategy seems to me to be essential if socialism is to have any future in Britain and elsewhere. But what I have tried to write about in this book seems to me to be even more fundamental, for it is about the very ethic of the socialist project itself. To summarize, perhaps inevitably too crudely, I would say that the trouble with socialism, and thus the trouble with socialists, has been a lack of humanity and of imagination.

The lack of humanity has always seemed obvious to me right from the time when I first became politically active through the Trotskyist movement in the early 1970s. Whether I became interested in psychoanalysis because of this experience is hard to tell; the irrationality of the organization I first belonged to was so rampant that I have little doubt that Freud would have had a marvellous time, had he been a member. What I found most striking about this experience was the way in which such socialists displayed so little interest in the individual. The mysteries of life and death, of feeling and passion, of dreaming and imagination, of love and terror – it was as if these things didn't exist. Yet, in terms of the life of the organizations to which I belonged, they were so obviously central to the real, as opposed to formal, dynamic of these peculiar human communities. It was as if one could only become politically committed by adhering to a shallow view of life and, although I have met and worked with many socialists since then whose depth of vision it has been a privilege to have encountered, the basic shallowness of the movement of which I have been a part remains incontrovertible.

For the past fifteen years then, whilst remaining politically engaged, I have also clung resolutely to the margins of a quite different tradition – psychoanalysis. To the extent that its objective is to enable us to lie to ourselves a little less than we do, psychoanalysis can sometimes seem like a merciless process of stripping away illusion. For any critical theory of society and culture, psychoanalysis should therefore be an obvious ally. However, no doubt because of its distinctive class location (and within Britain this location is expressed in an exaggerated spatial form through that locality lying within a two-mile radius of London's Swiss Cottage underground station) psychoanalysis contains its own immanent contradictions. Alongside its critical method it has developed its own distinctive blindness, its very own framework of myth and illusion. Psychoanalysis, to its adherents, offers both disturbance and consolation, and nowhere is this clearer than when it seeks to comprehend the world beyond the consulting room. A method which has proven so incisive when revealing the struggle between forces of life and death in the psyche seems quite incapable of discerning the same struggle for life and death in society. Only the threat of nuclear annihilation seems to have stirred some analysts into a partial form of political engagement. The outside world has otherwise seemed just too incomprehensible to warrant any form of commitment. Instead, to a world which seems primitive, dangerous and out of control, psychoanalysis has offered the consolation of a good enough personal redemption, a kind of stoical individualism immortalized through Freud's therapeutic aim of 'normal unhappiness'.

Yet, despite such shortcomings, psychoanalysis has managed to offer the most profound insights into what it means to be human. Although this may sound heretical, I have found the work of the post-Freudians – Klein,

Winnicott, Bion and latterly Meltzer – to be more revealing than the work
of Freud himself. The greatness of Freud lies in the fact that he constituted
the starting point of a movement which has grown and flourished for nearly
100 years. But it was Freud's followers, starting with Klein, who through
their work with children, infants and psychotics carried the psychoanalytic
gaze towards the basic core of subjectivity, from a concern with the
vicissitudes of the sexual impulse towards a focus upon the struggle for
psychical integration in the context of immanent catastrophe. Putting it
crudely, Klein heralds a shift within psychoanalysis from a phallocentric to
a mammocentric universe; from sexual desire and anxiety to ontological
desire and ontological insecurity.

The work of Klein, Winnicott and Bion is absolutely appropriate to our
times, given its coincidence with three contemporary debates: those concerned with feminism, the nuclear threat and post-modernism.

Whereas the classical psychoanalysis of Freud revolved around the
figure of the oedipal father, contemporary psychoanalysis centres upon the
mother – the first 'other' in terms of the child's development. In other words,
our first encounter with the world, and hence with ourselves, is mediated
through the presence of a woman who is capable of 'just being' with us.
Men find this so hard: just to be with baby without wanting constantly to
do things with baby; to be responsive and empathic, not just for a few hours
or days but for months and months. This culturally induced split between
maleness and femaleness, between doing and being, between containment
through projects, actions and objectives and self-containment, has been
charted with formidable thoroughness in recent years. Hence, in part, the
reason why so many feminists have been drawn towards psychoanalysis.

A second distinctive characteristic of post-Freudian psychoanalysis lies
in its shift away from Freud's earlier notion of drive conflict (sex and
aggression) towards his later notion of contradictory forces: Eros and
Thanatos, the life force and the death wish.

Winnicott, perhaps more than any other, focuses most fully upon the life
force: an expansive, desiring, integrative and hopeful force discernible in
all infants but, like an unfolding flower, so easily crushed. But it is to Bion
that we must look for the corresponding analysis of the death wish: an urge,
at work within individuals and groups alike, not to know, not to think, not
to develop; a kind of internally activated self-destruct mechanism lurking
within the human subject. This is not just an avoidance, a turning a blind

eye, but an attack on thinking itself and an attempt to live in a world of anti-thought.

The problem of 'false consciousness' becomes reframed in Bion's work as the problem of 'true consciousness'. In a world lacking any kind of integrity, how is truth-seeking possible? Psychoanalysis has been continually drawn towards seeking meaning, even in the worst recesses of human experience. In the 1950s, through the work of Bettelheim and others, it sought to comprehend the Holocaust. Today an increasing number of analysts – from Kovel (1983) on the Left fringe to Segal (1986) in the establishment centre – are seeking to make sense of our apparent equanimity in the face of nuclear genocide.

A third characteristic of post-Freudian psychoanalysis finds expression in its concern to chart the experience of personal disintegration common to the psychoses. This concern corresponds to the shift away from Freud's early model of instinctual tension and conflict towards the struggle between life and death within the psyche. It is a concern which runs closely parallel to that of cultural critics such as Fredric Jameson (1983) who have sought to understand the processes of cultural disintegration which appear to have gathered pace throughout the West during the closing decades of the twentieth century. God – the first casualty of modernization – was quickly followed by family, community and now perhaps class. Do we now live in a world without bonds or commitments? Post-modernism is a society without tradition, without a past, without continuity, reduced to modernizing the already modernized. Absent of meaning and absent of feeling, without time or space – how like the inner experience of psychosis it is.

These, then, are some of the most important resonances between contemporary psychoanalysis and current political and cultural issues. Modern social movements, particularly feminism, have sought to encompass the relationship between subjectivity and the social world through the phrase 'the personal is political'. But to my mind, if political and social thought is to come to terms in an adequate way with the contribution of psychoanalysis it needs to have the courage to go further than this. It needs to understand that the human being is not an infinitely malleable material but, conversely, that as corporeal beings we have a nature which is not only irreducible to social circumstance but itself is a nature capable of determination. The personal is, to some extent, political; but the political is also, to some extent, personal.

It is remarkable that political theories which claim to be materialist have for so long ignored the material reality of what it is to be human: to have a body, a body which develops and then decays; to have a psyche with its own laws of structuration and process. Here has been a huge lacuna in Marxist thinking. Do we really believe that from birth we are merely some kind of putty upon which social forces work? The crude determinism of this approach may now have been largely abandoned but the new variants, because of their greater sophistication, are perhaps even more dangerous. The new determinism allows for a certain recalcitrance; we are not moulded just like that. Society's imprint finds no direct reflection upon the psyche; rather, it undergoes processes of distortion, displacement and reconfiguration; so it leaves an image but not a one-to-one image. In political terms, such attitudes find expression in the theory of the 'cultural lag' – the idea that after a major social transformation many years will elapse before our human nature can be dragged into line with the newly transformed circumstances. More recently, certain strands within feminism have reinforced this attitude by reducing the question of gender purely to the social relations of reproduction, as if the human material itself is shapeless, androgenous.

Let us ask the question, then: are we the only natural phenomenon upon this earth with no 'grain'? Are there no tensions, fissures or fault lines within the material of the human psyche which deserve our respect and recognition? Marx was quite clear on this issue: without an attitude of respect for his material the labourer merely forces his will upon his subject matter and will produce a misshapened object, an effect he hadn't intended. And has Marxism not already produced its fair share of misshapened objects? Stalin and Pol Pot indicate where this doctrine of human malleability takes us.

This notion that the political is thoroughly and deeply personal is perhaps the one recurring theme throughout this book. I am using the word 'political' in its broadest sense as a synonym for a moral engagement with life; a form of engagement which, whilst exemplified by those directly and explicitly involved in political affairs, is one nevertheless shared by all whose sense of human value leads them, in whatever way, to take action. In other words, as I see it, politics is only partly about the behaviour of political parties; it constitutes the tip of the iceberg beneath which exists an entire political culture based upon the activities of groups, communities, clubs, religious and cultural organizations, trade unions, and so on. Seen in this light, countless thousands of individuals are engaged in an everyday struggle to transform the immediate environment in which they live, to remedy injustices, to create new social and cultural forms, to provide solidarity or mutual aid, to make things better.

This phrase, 'to make things better', seems to me to be the heart of the matter. It suggests to me an attitude to life which is fundamentally reparative. It is not about the pursuit of a perfect world, rather it is an attitude which recognizes the damage and injury daily incurred by the collective body of humanity (of which we are both victims and perpetrators) and a commitment to make amends. Take as an example two letters I find in my newspaper today. (the *Guardian*, 25 April 1989). One is a statement signed by six village chiefs from the Baram district of Sarawak. It refers to the recent mass arrests of villagers seeking to blockade logging routes in their area. Here are some extracts from their poignant letter to the West:

> For a long time we have suffered from the logging activities. Our forest resources have gone. Our food supply is reduced. The river waters are polluted. Our rice farms and fruit trees are damaged. The wild animals have run away. . . We are the poorest people in the country. We are the victims of logging, of people from the big modern outside world who don't understand our system or our rights. We just want to live like everybody else. . . So much land is already given to the timber companies. We just want a little for ourselves and to know that it is protected from loggers and other people. . . We are people with a proud culture and way of life that is based on our forest and land. Don't take our forest and culture and dignity away.

A second letter refers to the impact of NATO's low-flying training flights upon the Labrador community:

> I recently heard Chief Ashini speaking about the overflying, and the effect it has on the people in Labrador. The Innu people spend six months of the year out on the land, fishing, hunting and gathering. When the jets come over the shock and the noise is appalling. The caribou stampede; female mink and foxes eat their young. Families are traumatised – one camp was overflown 26 times in a single hour. In Europe the planes are not allowed to fly below 150 metres, but in Labrador they fly as low as 30 metres. . . The Innu people feel very isolated in their struggle. . .

It is said that we are civilized people, yet our savagery, brutality and indifference seem beyond our comprehension. It is this, perhaps more than anything else, that perplexes me and in a very personal way, not just as a problem 'out there' but also in terms of my own responses, my own inadequacy in facing up to the world in which I live. So this is a very personal book. It has been a way of thinking through the conflict I feel between the desire to lead a normal untroubled life and the need to sustain a sense of moral and political commitment. In thinking of the ways in which we avoid commitment I have had to face up to my personal culpability, my longing for comfort and routine, my unwillingness to confront through imagination the pain and suffering that this world is so full of. Some might say that this is no more than the writhing of a solitary liberal conscience. Well, let them console themselves this way. Although I speak as a white, middle-class man, I believe that most people, in Western countries, will find themselves in these pages somewhere. If I have a doubt, it is about my ability to articulate my thought and experience in a way which does justice to the issues I have sought to address.

Writing an introduction to this book has been hard: hard to sum up what I wished to say in what is perhaps this one chance I have been given. I have tried to speak from the heart; to write with precision and passion. But for me, at least, it does not come easily. I have been working on this for at least ten years and yet, now that I have finished, have done as much for the time being as I can, I have no sense of whether what I offer will affect you, the reader, in the way that I hope or whether it will seem naive, childish even.

Of course my narcissism gets in the way; it tempts me to believe that what I have produced is, if not perfect, then at least without precedent. It is a very personal book and, I suppose, that is my fear – that it says more about me than you or, rather, us. In the past I often used to write under a pseudonym. I have been tempted to do the same here; it might save me much embarrassment. On the other hand, it might give me the divine pleasure of being the author of an anonymous best seller. I keep wondering whether this tendency of mine to reveal myself in print is some kind of weird disorder, a strange kind of exhibitionism.

I know such thoughts seem petty but it seems right that you, the reader, should have no illusions about the subject of this book. In order to write this thing I have had to take a couple of years off from what I regard as a real engagement with this world. I feel a strong need now to get back in, to take the plunge, to practise what I preach – a politics of the imagination.

Not so long ago I read about a prisoner in Uruguay. He had been imprisoned by the Stroessner dictatorship some twenty years ago. For many of those years he has been in solitary confinement. The regime would not set him free, nor would they let him die. To symbolize their power over this human voice they had embarked upon a final act to crush this prisoner's being. They ripped out the door of his cell and bricked him in completely, presumably leaving a small hatch for his food to be passed through and his slops to be received.

I meant to keep the newspaper article as a reminder, as something to turn to when life was becoming too comfortable. That I forgot says, not just something about me, but something about all of us, about the thousand little ways in which we accommodate ourselves to the intolerable. If, in reading this book, just a few people will have been helped towards a renewed political commitment then it will have been worth the effort. As to the nature of that commitment, well, this is what I hope much of this book is about.

2

The Art of the Possible

Most of this chapter was written more than ten years ago. It is an attempt to explore the subversive potential of human subjectivity, the phenomenom Winnicott refers to as 'creativity' – an engagement with reality, internal and external, which extends, rather than diminishes, human possibilities. I wish to suggest that such an attitude to life can be best pictured through the idea of a permanent dialogue, a dialogue between self and one's objects.[1] By engaging in the dialogue with such objects one can act imaginatively, make use of what the human and physical environment offers, critically examine ideas, feelings or situations, create and destroy, play and explore, give and receive.

What follows is, then, an attempt to understand such forms of subversive engagement with reality, an orientation to life which is all too infrequently nurtured in the home and rarely, if ever, in the school. It is also an attempt to understand some of the forces, internal and external, which stand opposed to it. Above all, I suppose, this is a plea to people to put such an ethic more centrally within their own lives in all of its settings.

A SENSE OF 'PERMANENT POSSIBILITY'

The creativity that we are studying belongs to the approach of the individual to external reality. . . Contrasted with this is a relationship with external reality which is one of compliance, the world and its details being recognized but only as something to be fitted in with or demanding adaptation. . . In a tantalizing way many

individuals have experienced just enough of creative living to rec-
ognize that for most of their time they are living uncreatively, as if
caught up in the creativity of someone else, or of a machine.
(Winnicott, 1974, p. 76)

How does an individual develop and maintain a sense of 'the possible'; a durable internal conviction that reality can be changed, that 'the given' can be subverted? And how do we block ourselves from developing this sense? These kinds of questions were to haunt me for several years during the late 1970s and early 1980s. For it was at this time that it slowly became clear to the Left that crisis and recession were bringing to the West not revolution but despair and fatalism. What was happening to us at this time? Why were we losing any sense of possibility, that sense which had been so urgent and so living in the previous decade?

During this period it was often said that what people lacked was a vision of a different future, of socialism perhaps. Whilst this is probably true the problem is much deeper than this, for what constrains us most is not so much this absence of a necessarily distant vision but the lack of an idea of how even tomorrow might be different. 'How else could things be?' people often say. This orientation to life was clearly fuelled and supported by a political culture such as Thatcherism, but it was not created by this culture. There is something more timeless about it. This numbing sense of same-ness, of routine, of 'the given', stands as the antithesis to that orientation which Winnicott calls 'creativity'. Henry Miller captures it thus:

Just now and then, someone comes. . . undone, as it were, from the meaningless glue in which we are all stuck – the rigmarole we call everyday life and which is not life but a trance-like suspension above the great stream of life. (*Sexus*, p. 117)

To understand this I found that I had to turn to my own experience. What was this glue of everyday reality and its rhythms; its uncanny ability to shut out anything disturbing which might intrude into my own life? What were those forces within me that didn't want to face difficult truths, didn't want to learn and didn't want change? I had to consider both the power of imagination and its denial – fantasy and its seductive embrace – in my life. I had to consider the manifold routes through which I rendered myself irresponsible by putting comfort, certainty and routine before risk and disturbance.

I shall begin by sharing with you my experience of fantasy; the bit of the glue that I most frequently used to get immersed in.

MORBID AND SUBVERSIVE FANTASY

On the one hand there is 'routine'; on the other, 'the possible'. Common sense is on the side of routine – after all, anything else is just wishful thinking, sheer fantasy. We should not, however, slip into thinking that fantasy and common sense somehow stand opposed to each other, for one cannot discover possibilities through fantasy. Fantasy takes us nowhere; that is its purpose. We fantasize when masturbating, naturally; for here the thought and the action take us away from the real. We cannot act upon fantasies. Fantasy is not concerned with the possible, for possibility is intertwined with reality and with its subversion. Fantasy belongs to sheer abstraction, to disembodied thought, to thought dissociated from action, to thought frozen in abstraction, to 'if only', to helpless longing. Fantasy belongs to the realm of impossibility. It cannot be subversive – unlike imagination, which always is.

Maybe this argument has been a bit too ruthless. For there is one sense in which fantasy can be subversive. It can subvert terror. Many families, schools, religious institutions and clubs order children to be pure. Think of a family in a small town that attends church regularly; that turns off the television when smutty films come on; whose sons attend Cubs and go to Sunday School. For an adolescent in this context to have a fantasy about the girl next door or his sister or a boy at the Cubs, which is 'carnal' in nature is to be subversive. Within any social order that directs us not to think certain things, it is subversive to dare to think these unthinkable thoughts, even if the thought is idle, of the nature of daydream and fantasy. In such contexts, to think the unthinkable in itself is to be defiant: to say 'no'; to assert one's autonomy, one's own desire, one's own being. Is this defiance to be considered as shallow merely because it is dissociated from action?

The answer perhaps lies in the question of its effectiveness. What effect does this act of defiance have? Certainly it does not modify or destroy the social nexus itself; the parents do not give in. Indeed, if they knew what was going on in their son's mind, they would be outraged. In the face of such fantasy the effectiveness of terror can never be complete. Through his fantasy the child remains partially unbowed, refuses to comply totally. Fantasy, then, is defensive, a little indulgence we allow ourselves; a little space that terror cannot see, a space from which the ruling hand is quietly mocked. Terror, if it knew of this little space, would find it most offensive, this adolescent with his 'perverted' fantasies. We have then an 'offensive' defence; an immoral little practice.

Terror succeeds only if it forces you to appreciate it; to take its directives and proscriptions as your own; to adopt its morality and ethics. Then and only then does it inhabit our every little space. 'Perverted fantasy' is a moral reply to terror: the pervert as the moralist. This kind of fantasy is subversive, it relates to reality by defying it.

But here we have its limitation. It can only be of the moral order, and can only be in the nature of a defence. There is a danger to such fantasy, too. Pure terror needs perversity to feed off. It must have it, otherwise it cannot flourish. Purity anticipates, begs for, perversity. In the last analysis, if this fantasy remains divorced from action nothing changes. We must terrorize the terrorists: actions speak louder than words; words louder than thoughts; thoughts louder than silence. Can subversive fantasy become translated into action or is it basically idle?

We have spoken so far only of the form of fantasy through which an individual asserts her or his autonomy, but most fantasy is not like this. There is another kind of fantasy, much more widespread, a kind Winnicott speaks of in his article 'Dreaming, fantasying and living'. Speaking of this kind of fantasying Winnicott (1974, p. 31), says: '[it] remains an isolated phenomenon, absorbing energy but not contributing in either to dreaming or to living'.

This kind of fantasying is associated with dissociation (a form of splitting) rather than with repression. We are quite conscious of it, and it often inhabits a huge space in which we place ourselves to have adventures. But it is not a part of our being: it is a place we fly to, an area of non-being. In a very rich phrase, Winnicott suggests that one can see 'the relationship between fantasying and the abandonment of hope in (object) relating' (1974, p. 33). Imagination is the vehicle of hope; fantasy the vehicle of despair.

Take an example. You see me in a room. I appear to be reading a book. However, upon closer examination it becomes clear that I am staring at the page, not reading it. I am lost in fantasy. I am not reading the book nor am

I in this room: I am presenting a paper on The epistemological false premisses of Lacan's theory of the self' to a packed conference somewhere in Paris (in spring). I am not where you think I am. I am absent.

In such fantasy all things are possible, thus its appeal. Fantasy soars above necessity, knowing of nothing so mundane. It is therefore an *unfreedom* which passes itself off as the freedom to do anything. It is a form of omnipotence based, as all omnipotence is, upon actual helplessness. Fantasy is the narcissist's stuff of life – he loses himself within it, and without it he is lost.

Winnicott argues that fantasy has no symbolic value. If I were to tell an analyst of a fantasy I was in the middle of when in his room, there would be no interpretation he could make of it. For, Winnicott argues, the unconscious speaks through dream but not through fantasy. Fantasies have no double meanings or over-determinations; they have no richness or depth. Rather, they are superficial, distracting, noisy. When I fantasize, I am becoming withdrawn and I enter a self-containing narcissistic universe.

Take another example. I am walking down a country lane in early March. The air is still, it is quiet, the land lies melancholy and grey. However, I am taking none of this in. Only occasionally do I appreciate the passing trees, the sun's light playing on the damp road; for I am busy elsewhere, lost in fantasy, having adventures. I am not lost in thought, for these are not thoughts; there is no movement in them. These thoughts are not moving anywhere, they have no direction and no movement, they are lifeless things.

Because in fantasy anything is possible, it provides a kind of excitement. In fantasy things happen 'just like that' ('now I am commandeering a boat from moorings somewhere near Chichester, escaping on it out to sea; avoiding the attempt of the military government to capture me – a few moments later I have reached Normandy'). Things appear to whiz, shoot, slither, rush, leap in rapid succession. (How many times in fantasy have I leaped to fame!) But in reality, nothing moves, everything is frozen. I am motionless. There is some depth in fantasy, then; it is something that appears vigorous but in essence is lifeless. This dead thing which appears to live, which seduces, induces, beckons, whispers, invites us to slip back. This little dead pervert has set itself up in another's home, sits in the owner's armchair, gobbles up his food.

There is another respect in which fantasy has some depth. When lost in fantasy we are unable to take anything in. We are no longer receptive to the real world in which we exist. We therefore cannot enrich ourselves by using sensuous objects around us; rather, we attempt to live off our own content: we attempt to conjure our own excitements. To use the bodily analogy, fantasy is the psychical equivalent of sick, shit or spittle (physical contents we externalize) wrapped up in such a way that it looks for all the world like an appetizing chocolate bar. Here then is the second respect in which fantasy has a certain depth – it is a waste product which passes itself off as enrichment.

How can we compare the two forms of fantasy, the subversive and the morbid? Subversive fantasy is an expression of autonomy but not of agency. Through his carnal adventures the adolescent clings to life in the face of a force that would have him renounce his life in favour of another's (the life his parents desire for him). Subversive fantasy is an expression of helplessness but not of hopelessness; the fantasy is in the way of an expression of hope. It is an offensive defence, a coarse gesture, the 'fingers up' to terror. Morbid fantasy on the other hand is inoffensive: it offends only the person who is seduced into it. Only when the other has intruded into our every little space, only then does morbid fantasy dominate. The more we put into this kind of fantasy, the more we dissociate ourselves from our own life. The more terror forces us to give up our own life, our own desire, the more we become essentially absent, on leave. Rather than being in possession of life, we become possessed by dead things, dead images.

Let people have their harmless dreams of love, of fame, of fortune. We have a whole industry now devoted to providing the lifeless matter on which fantasy thrives: film, television, magazines, novels, comics. Everyday life is becoming increasingly narcissistic, marked by a real withdrawal from living, a growing lifelessness. Of course we have our laughs, but no real joy: 'Joy is a kind of ecstatic bleeding, a disgraceful sort of super-contentment which overflows from every pore of your being. . . to be joyous is to be a madman in a world of sad ghosts' (Miller, 1966, p. 31).

IMAGINATION

Winnicott compares fantasy and imagination thus:

> The patient may sit in her room and while doing nothing except breathing she has (in her fantasy) painted a picture, or she has done an

interesting piece of work in her job, or she has been for a country walk;
but from the observer's point of view nothing whatever has happened.
In fact, nothing is likely to happen. . . On the other hand, she may be
sitting in her room thinking of tomorrow's job and making plans, or
thinking about her holiday, and this may be an imaginative exploration
of the world and of the place where dream and life are the same thing.
(1974, p. 32)

Whilst psychoanalysis, particularly for Winnicott and Rycroft, frequently
addresses itself to an analysis of imagination, it often tends to do so in an
oblique manner. Perhaps it is because imaginative human activity is so
everyday and normal that psychoanalysis has tended to shun it. A theory
of 'the irrational' perhaps feels no concern for something which is apparently so conscious and purposeful. If this is the case, it is psychoanalysis's
loss; for, as we shall see, there are a number of points at which a complete
theory of imaginative action must draw upon psychoanalytical insight for
its realization.

   We must therefore look elsewhere for the foundation of a theory of the
imagination; in fact, to Marx and his theory of the labour process. For Marx,
imaginative activity was the very essence of humanness. It was the process
by which, through natural human production, subjectivity transcends the
given, and new physical objects appear in a world which is increasingly a
human creation. This process, through which the 'not yet' becomes the
'present', the possible becomes the actual, Marx calls 'objectification'. It is
the process through which human objects come to be. It is important at this
point to understand that Marx's discussion of 'objectification' occurs within
a set of rationalist parameters; he is not speaking of objects in the psychoanalytic sense. As we shall see, an object such as a tool or instrument has
a double status: as a real physical object with demonstrable properties and
as a psychical object with particular meanings for the person who uses it.

   The classic statement on the role of the imagination is given by Marx in
an attempt to provide a specific characterization of productive labour. The
theme he develops here had already been sketched in a similar vein in the
introduction to the *Grundrisse*, specifically in that section which outlines the
dialectic of production and consumption (Marx, 1857/8, pp. 81–111). But it
is in the first volume of *Capital* (1876) where the theme becomes more
elaborate. We will cite Marx's most well-known summary statement in full,
for this will provide us with the opportunity to distil some of its elements:

What distinguishes the worst architect from the best of bees is this, that the architect raises his structure in *imagination* before he erects it in reality. At the end of every labour-process, we get a result that already existed in the imagination of the labourer at its commencement. He not only effects a change of form in the material on which he works, but he also realises a purpose of his own that gives the law to his modus operandi, and to which he must subordinate his will. . . the process demands that, during the whole operation, the workman's will be steadily in consonance with his purpose. (1876, p. 174)

The first thing to realize is that imaginative activity occurs within a boundary set by two objects: on the one hand, the idea that the individual has, which provides the starting point for activity; on the other, the actual product, the finishing point of this activity. On the one hand is the object(ive) of production; on the other, the finished object. The labour process therefore describes a movement from the conceived to the real(ized) object of production, from the psychical to the physical, from imagination to reality (Colletti, 1972, pp. 82–92).

Secondly Marx speaks of the 'material' of production – a material with its own laws and regularities which constitute its recalcitrance. Not that such laws manifest themselves to us in an unmediated way. At a given moment in history we are only able to grasp the particular forms in which they present themselves.

Society is always faced with the same laws of nature. Its existing historical structure determines the form in which men are subjected to these laws, their mode of operation, their field of application, and the degree to which they can be understood and made socially useful. (Schmidt, 1971, p. 98)

A fast-moving river, for example, will always impose certain constraints upon human purpose but, whereas a primitive society will behold in the river's energy only its limitations, our society tends only to see its own possibilities.

Of course the matter to be worked upon may be human or non-human, according to whether one is engaged in what Marx calls 'material production' or 'the production of social relationships'. Again there is no neat separation between the two. All forms of collective material production are also, simultaneously, productions of social relationships. As we shall see, irrespective of the nature of the material of production, the key property is its recalcitrance. Because it imposes constraints upon the realization of need and desire, it limits our independence and autonomy. In other words, it shows us that we are dependent and interdependent beings.

The third element of the labour process is the instrument of the labourer or the tool. As Marx says: 'An instrument of labour is a thing, or complex of things, which the labourer interposes between himself and the subject of his labour, and which serves as the conductor of his activity' (1876, p. 174). The tool, like the material of production, may assume a variety of forms. It may be an inert physical instrument (a chisel or piano) or, at the other extreme, it may assume the complex social form of a human organization. The central point, however, is that, whatever the forms, the instrument exists as something external to the individual. It therefore confronts the individual with its recalcitrance in a manner analogous to the material of production. As Marx notes, the ability to use tools is a second distinguishing characteristic of humankind. However, Marx never considers this ability in its developmental setting, that is, from the point of view of the developing child. If we do so, we can begin to see how the ability to handle means of production is essential to any form of giving.

The ability to give assumes an ability to handle such 'means'. There has to be some means by which we give. In the first instance we use aspects of our own physical being as 'means'. The infant learns to use its face as a medium for giving; it learns how to show concern or affection; it learns how to use its voice as a means for making certain sounds through which it might give of itself; it learns how to use its muscles as a means for giving – for hugging, for offering, for making things, for moving towards things. The human musculature, the voice and so on, are given the general term 'effectors' by modern psychology; bodily instruments, such as the ears and the eyes, which are designed primarily to receive from the environment are not surprisingly called 'receptors'.

The human body is therefore the first instrument that the human being makes use of. This is true genetically and phylogenetically. But as an instrument, it stands apart from our own subjectivity and, like other more obviously external instruments such as machines, telescopes and cars, of which it is the prototype, it has a certain 'objective' quality. We can use or abuse our body as an object, just as we can use or abuse any other object which is external to us.

Thus parts of the body constitute the first human instruments. Before the infant can learn to use any tool, it must learn of the possibilities and constraints of its own body. The physical attributes of the body can be harnessed to realize possibilities that the infant might conceive of. We are so used to speech, to hand movements and so on, that we overlook the fact that they are themselves productions: in fact, the most elementary but essential of all human productions. The infant has an idea of the kind of sound it would like to make and it makes use of its voice-box (instrument) to operate upon breath (material) to produce sounds (product). The infant can treat its productions as something external to itself. However, not all externalizations are productions. As we shall see in later chapters, many externalizations, including much of what passes for human communication, are no more than attempts at dumping, depositing or projecting noxious psychical material into others. Externalizations which assume the distinctive form of human productions enjoy the property of having some degree of separateness; thus they can be considered, enjoyed and identified with or disparaged and attacked. There is no difference between the nature of the process involved in the infant's babbling and the nature of the process involved in, say, artistic production. The artist may have an idea of the kind of mark she would like to make on her canvas: the fingers/hands/arm musculature and the brush constitute the means, the paint, the material and the brush mark the product.

Of course, it is not always the case that the infant has an idea of the kind of sound it would like to make before making it nor does the artist always have an idea of the brush mark. Although the infant may produce sounds, very often its productions will be the outcome of exploration and improvisation rather than of purpose – a crucial distinction, as we shall later see.

The final element in the labour process is the labourer. A person whose capacity to imagine – to use objects, to construct, repair and destroy through the use of love, gratitude and aggression – can, as we have noted, by no means be assumed. In consideration of the subjective element in the labour process we shall find that psychoanalysis has probably more to offer us than Marxism. Indeed this entire chapter may be taken as an attempt to suggest that there is a point at which psychoanalysis and Marxism actually do share the same object, and can therefore be treated as commensurate discourses. It is Marx, however, who notes a vital element in the labourer's subjectivity which psychoanalysis overlooks. The labour process begins with an idea: the idea of the individual which defines his purpose. This idea

is, then, the starting point for his productive activity. But this idea is more
than just his starting point for, as Marx puts it, the idea 'gives the law' to his
activity, a law to which he must subordinate his will. Marx continues:

> And this subordination is no mere momentary act. . . the process de-
> mands that, during the whole operation, the workman's will be steadily
> in consonance with his purpose. This means close attention. The less he
> is attracted by the nature of the work and the mode in which it is carried
> on and the less, therefore, he enjoys it as something which gives play to
> his bodily and mental powers, the more close his attention is forced to
> be. (1876, p. 174)

The idea, then, not only begins the process of imaginative production, but
also is its constant guide and companion. Note also the essentially hedonistic character of the labour involved: if the activity is not in itself enjoyable,
then the possibility that the end-product fails to reflect one's original intent
is much greater. Applied to the realm of political action, we might ask how
 often our subjective experience of politics in either mass reformist or
revolutionary organizations 'gives play to our bodily and mental powers'.
In my experience this occurs only very rarely. It is not that politics should
be pleasurable in the narrow sense of 'fun'. (In times like these, politics can
be a profoundly depressing, painful and at times dangerous form of
activity.) But even when things are going badly, we must seek a hedonistic
base to our involvement: our activity must be something which develops
our own possibilities – our powers of feeling, of imagination, of wonder-
ment. If it does not, the organization in which one participates will feed off
the powerlessness of its membership. The division between leaders and
led must start to be broken down here and now; overcoming this division
must be an integral part of the creation of the instrument to end class rule.

To return, finally, to Marx's model of the labour process, we can see how
the idea which defines the labourer's purpose determines his activity and,
in this manner, he becomes self-determining. Marx's picture of the labour
process therefore discloses the manner in which action is both determined
and self-determining; it is both an acknowledgement of autonomy and a
recognition of dependence.

THE BAD WORKMAN

Through his model of the labour process, Marx has provided us with an account of imaginative activity which resembles an ideal-type formation. If all goes well, this is how human beings become productive beings. It is a rationalist model which certainly allows for things going wrong, but within its terms they would go wrong for a good reason. We may choose an instrument which is inadequate for the material to be worked upon: a blunt chisel to work on mahogany; a bureaucratic party to bring about the revolution. We may fail to recognize the particular form in which the laws and regularities of our raw material appears to us (an endemic difficulty for Marxism) or we may lack the attentiveness necessary for us to transform the material in a way which is consonant with our purpose. For any of these reasons imaginative action may founder.

The trouble with Marx's model is that it assumes an essentially benign and reasonable subject, but what if things are not quite like this? The power of psychoanalysis stems from its assumption that the human subject is often quite unreasonable, indeed at times is quite perverse. Psychoanalysis provides us with a way of looking at how aspects of our own subjectivity prevent us from becoming fully human agents, capable of using objects to change the externally given. It can disclose to us the site of a number of internal forces which stand opposed to the realization of possibility.

The point about Marx's picture of a natural labour process – the process of imaginative, purposeful production – is that it assumes the existence of a subject, the labourer, capable of using objects. Psychoanalysis, on the other hand, shows us that this cannot simply be assumed, that it is a developmental capacity which is acquired only with some difficulty, and even then it is only ever achieved in a 'more or less' fashion. We noted before the distinction to be made between 'psychical objects' and real objects. At first, the infant lives in a world consisting almost entirely of the former. Here the phantasy[2] status of the object is paramount and its status as something having a reality in its own right is minimal. Winnicott speaks of the infant, at this stage, having a cavalier attitude towards its real objects. In particular, the nurturing figure is taken totally for granted, treated as if it had no life of its own. The figure, in turn, supports this illusion by its adaptiveness, by always being on hand and capable of anticipating or empathizing.

At this stage, the stage of object-relating, 'the subject allows certain alterations in the self to take place, of a kind that has caused us to invent the term cathexis' (Winnicott, 1974, p. 103). The object has become meaningful. But, Winnicott adds, if the object is to be used (that is, engaged with in some way which is purposeful) then it 'must necessarily be real in the sense of being part of shared reality, not a bundle of projections' (ibid.). The point, however, is that our objects never cease also having the characteristic of being a bundle of projections, and this is true irrespective of whether the object in question is one's lover, comrade, boss, the group to which one belongs, or an object of production such as a musical instrument, a theoretical framework or a magazine.

We therefore always maintain a dual relationship with our objects, and their phantastic quality always threatens to undermine their real and actual status. I now examine the role of envy, the unconscious phantasy life it gives rise to and the way in which it disrupts the imaginative process.

Narcissistic Hatred

By now it should be clear that the path from an idea to its realization is littered with constraints. Both the instrument or tool and the material of production confront the subject with their own recalcitrance. A woman sits before a piano. She may have an idea of what it is that she wishes to produce but she cannot realize this idea instantaneously: the piano stands between her idea and its realization. She must engage with this instrument, recognize that it will not simply comply with her intentions, and find some way of overcoming the constraints that it imposes. Thus, for example, she may find that no single note will actually invoke one of the sounds she seeks to realize, and thus she endeavours to seek a chord which will do the trick. By engaging with the instrument in this way, she transcends the limitations it imposes. But this transcendence is based upon a prior recognition of necessity: she adopts an attitude of respect, a position of humility before the recalcitrant partner in her musical endeavour.

As imaginative beings, we are reminded of our neediness by both the material and the instrument of production: we need them to realize our idea. They therefore disclose to us our own lack and incompleteness, our dependence upon our environment and the everyday objects we have created from it. But what if we are unwilling or unable to accept ourselves as dependent, needy, imperfect or incomplete? What if we are unable to relate to the natural world with a sense of humility or respect? This is the dilemma of the narcissist and one that psychoanalysis has charted with formidable thoroughness.

The concept of envy was introduced into contemporary psychoanalysis by Melanie Klein (Klein, 1957). Whilst one may disagree with the particular way in which Klein construes envy – as others have noted, at times it almost takes on the status of 'original sin' in her work – one cannot deny the power of this unconscious process in mental life. The following example may illustrate its mode of operation.

About twelve years ago, when small fascist organizations in Britain were still quite strong, I was struck by something I saw on children's television one Saturday. A group of actors were being filmed live from a council estate in north London; the idea was to present a piece of participative slapstick. There was an enormous tank of water and hundreds of plastic buckets. Those present had to throw as much water at each other as they could in the space of a few minutes – local residents were specifically invited to join in. Amongst the local residents were a group of skinheads, who were, and still are, the main recruiting ground for extra-parliamentary fascist groups. I watched with fascination as the event got underway. At first it was great fun, but as the excitement mounted the skinheads started to look increasingly awkward, clumsy, self-conscious and then aggressive. Eventually it became clear that they were no longer playing; they thought they were still being funny but others were becoming anxious. The 'water fight' had become more of a fight than a game; they were spoiling others' fun. At about that time, skinheads had developed the habit of breaking up punk concerts, mostly concerts given by bands they supported. I remember Siouxsie of The Banshees commenting sadly how skinheads seemed unable to let anyone have a good time without spoiling things. I suddenly began to see how skinhead culture resembled a 'culture of envy'.

According to Klein, envy occurs when the things you most desire for yourself are the things you most relentlessly attack. They are attacked precisely because they are needed. The skinhead watches others at play, being happy, getting excited, and feels an absence, a longing which reminds him of his own lack. Envy is both a desperate attempt to deny this sense of lack and an attack upon the thing which prompts it. It is an attempt to deny that there could be anything 'out there' that could be desirable. It is a refusal to recognize that there is a source of anything good beyond one's own (individual or group) subjectivity. As Bion (1957a) notes, the flip-side of envy is arrogance, the sense that there is nothing beyond what one already knows, has felt or experienced; indeed, there is nothing beyond self.

This is a kind of narcissism and a form of self-containment which is not freedom but its very opposite: one is contained within the limitations of one's own self. One cannot need, for the longing is unbearable; one cannot use objects effectively, for to do so one must accept their recalcitrance and one's own dependence on them. For this reason such a person cannot love, for to accept that another has something he might have need of would cause him to feel desolate. For this reason, also, such narcissistic types tend to be 'bad workmen', for if the objects around them dare present any obstacles to the realization of their ideas they will attack and spoil them (in other words, quarrel with them) with the utmost hatred. Thus Henry Miller speaks of an acquaintance who happened to be a pianist:

> He'd play it [the piano] with all his heart as if he were giving a concert. But maybe a third of the way through he'd stumble. Silence. He'd go back a few measures, break it down, build it up, slow, fast, one hand, two hands, all together, hands, feet, knuckles, elbows, moving forwards like a tank corps, sweeping everything before him, mowing down trees, hedges, fences, barns, walls. It was agonising to follow him. He was not playing for enjoyment – he was playing to perfect his technique. . . always advancing, progressing, attacking, conquering, annihilating, mopping up, realigning his forces, throwing out sentries and sentinels, covering his rear. . . (1966, p. 288)

Its not, therefore, that the narcissist is incapable of imaginative production but that the productions arise almost incidentally out of a desire to create a perfect internal object world. Instead of an attitude of respect towards the other on whom we depend to realize our ideas, the instrument is attacked precisely because of our dependence on it, him or her. There is no sense of partnership but instead an arrogant attitude of mastery.

Such an arrogant and omniscient attitude towards one's objects is clearly given support by a culture within which money is considered a universal good. Money's most essential property lies in its promise to overcome all obstacles, it is therefore a denial of the necessary recalcitrance of real objects. Marx (1844) spoke of money as 'the pimp' between man's need and his object. The pimp does not so much create new needs as grovel before existing ones. But because the pimp is 'so willing', the need that is serviced becomes corrupted – the needy person no longer has to work or struggle. Take prostitution as an example. The client can avoid the arduous work involved in dating and courting, he (I assume most clients are male) need no longer be haunted by concern about how the other values him, his appearance, his temperament, his achievements. He need no longer experience nagging and unbearable doubt as to the other's recalcitrance or refusal. In this sense the other ceases even to be *an object* of desire (for, as Balint (1979) notes, one of the original Greek senses of the work 'object' related to its status as a 'possible obstacle').

No work is required on behalf of the client other than that involved in the monetary transaction; no concern is necessary as to the other's sense of value. Indeed one may find relief in the knowledge that the other values only one's money. No doubt is involved, no element of chance. Money is indeed a magical thing. Its power of command is so immense that, without it, one is helpless and dependent.

Again, Marx's notes, 'The power of money in bourgeois society', are seminal in this context (1844, pp.165–70). Need no longer requires realization through imaginative action. One may be weak but money provides one with the appearance of strength. When one needs solace money promises to provide comfort. When one is lonely money can provide one with the appearance of companionship. When one feels empty money can provide one with the appearance of mystery. Money promises to transform every weakness, every lack into its opposite. Money is negation.

Money grants omnipotence. No possibility of refusal exists: money states one's rights and the other's obligations. Marx, in his parable of the 'Architect and the bee' (1876), describes the way in which need normally finds realization through use of the imagination. The architect raises his construction in his imagination and then finds the material and means with which to make real this conception. Money abolishes the 'gap' between need and its realization and thereby abolishes the imagination. Money enables a person to realize need instantly. To use Winnicott's terms, money fixes the individual in the realm of fantasy.

DESIRE AND THE NEW

> *An animal only produces what it immediately needs for itself and*
> *its young. It produces one-sidedly, whilst man produces univer-*
> *sally. It produces only under the dominion of immediate physical*
> *need, whilst man produces even when he is free from physical*
> *need and only truly produces in freedom therefrom. An animal*
> *produces only itself, whilst man reproduces the whole of nature.*
> *(Marx, 1844, p. 113)*

We have, then, two realms of human production, of imagination. One refers
to the realm of necessary activity based upon felt need; the other to the
realm of activity free from internal necessity – the realm of human desire.
Need and desire are not discrete; they are intimately related. This is the case
from the earliest stage of infancy, as Freud (1905) indicates through his idea
of their 'anaclitic relationship'. As Marx makes clear, in the passage above,
the distinction between need and desire lies in their relationship to freedom, specifically in the distinction between two forms of freedom: 'freedom
from', on the one hand; 'freedom to', on the other. 'Freedom to' – the true
realm of freedom of which Marx speaks – appears like a form of human
energy which is not based upon need and yet is a truly human (as opposed
to animal) form of experience. We have, therefore, a form of human energy,
an inner propulsion which is not based on a sense of insufficiency, for it
blossoms only in the absence of the experience of neediness. It is a 'drive'
which, far from being the outcome of lack, is the outcome of surfeit. And
whilst a sense of longing accompanies such desire, it is a longing to give,
to externalize an inner fullness.

In the case of both need and desire our imagination is prompted by an
absence. According to Bion (1962), the idea always refers to 'no-thing'. But
in the case of need this idea refers to 'something that is known but missing'
– food perhaps or warmth. In the case of desire, however, the idea refers
to 'something which has not yet existed', to something new. It may be a
building, a piece of music, a garden or a child's pullover. Whatever it is, so
long as it emerges from the producer's own subjectivity, then it will contain
within it something new. A thousand children could sit before the same
flower, but each would paint something different.

An architect may conceive of a building the likes of which has never been seen before; through her imagination she can produce an object which is quite novel. The thing she conceives of is, then, without precedent; it does not yet exist as an object anywhere in the world. Michael Balint suggests we use the term 'pre-object' to describe the content of the architect's imagination at this point (1979, p. 25). The labour which then transforms these pre-objects into real sensuous external objects is truly a form of creative activity, a labour of love pregnant with possibilities.

The question we must now ask is, 'Where do new ideas come from?' I do not at this point wish to go over the well-ploughed ground of Marxist analyses which show, to my mind convincingly, the relationship between a new form of consciousness and the historical conditions which provide its necessary setting. What I would like to do is to focus on the subjective moment of this phenomenon because, although the conditions prevailing provide the necessary ground for the appearance of the new, they are not a sufficient explanation in and of themselves. Crises, for example, require re-evaluation and an imaginative leap. If this, at some point, does not occur, the possibilities inherent within the situation will not become our possibilities; the necessary historical conditions for the unprecedented will not be sufficient. To cite Balint:

> The subject is on his own and his main concern is to produce something out of himself; this something to be produced may be an object but it is not necessarily so. I propose to call this the level or area of creation. The most often discussed example is, of course, artistic creation, but other phenomena belong to the same group, among them mathematics and philosophy, gaining insight, understanding something or somebody. (1979, p. 24)

It is not enough, then, to leave the issue of the origin of new ideas simply to the mercy of historical conditions; the subjective element is a determining factor in its own right and has been neglected by Marxism for too long.

Much of the rest of this chapter is an exploration of creativity, this capacity to go beyond the given to create something entirely new, without precedent. Later I examine the process of improvisation and our related ability to listen to our objects when, so to speak, they 'answer back' to us. But now I would like to consider the less improvisational aspect of creativity. Specifically I wish to look at the question I have already posed: 'Considered subjectively where do new ideas – in music, politics, philosophy – come from?' I wish to argue that they come from a creative cycle, essentially one of aggressive attack, play and reconstruction. First, then, we must examine the role of aggression in thought.

Gramsci's terms 'critical' and 'acritical' applied to the activity of thought and consciousness do no more than to give a name to something which classical Marxism focused on repeatedly. For example, in his *Philosophical Notebooks*, Lenin (1961) attacks the idea that for thought to be accurate it must necessarily remain faithful to the appearance of the thing it seeks to analyse. Things are in fact seldom as they seem. Thought that remains content to rest at the level of the appearance of things is guilty of a fundamental confusion, for 'the natural principle or the beginning, which is the starting point. . . is taken as the true. . . It is correct that people begin with that, but truth lies not in the beginning but in the end, or rather, in the continuation' (1961, p. 171). Thought must continually seek to get to the bottom of things, to cut through the obvious, to interrogate constantly what seems commonsensical. If thought is acritical, it remains passive, fixed at the level of the initial impression, without movement, lifeless. Subversive thought begins, above all, with one's own assumptions; it must constantly assume the form of an interrogation. As Fanon (1967) movingly puts it, in the final page of his *Black Skin, White Masks*:

> My final prayer
> O my body, make of me a man who always questions!

Again, psychoanalysis can aid our investigation here, for one of its distinctive features is the way in which it roots all intellectual functions in the body. In particular it draws attention to the way in which one of the earliest bodily functions – feeding – constitutes the prototype of later, more sophisticated psychical processes (Freud, 1925). For, even in the earliest days of its life, the infant demonstrates that it is capable of forming judgements: the feeding infant may either take in milk or refuse it. Even at this stage, then, it shows that it cannot be taken for granted. A moment's consideration suggests that the way in which we talk about our own thought processes betrays their bodily origins. We speak of something as giving 'food for thought'; we 'digest' new information; we 'chew something over' in our mind; there are some things we might read in a newspaper that we 'refuse to swallow', and so on.

Using this analogy, we can see how uncritical thought swallows things too easily. There is no element of refusal in it, no sense of aggression.

Moreover, very often uncritical consciousness is not just a result of one's own irresponsible lethargy; it is the sign of a form of consciousness which has been colonized by another. To refer back to our early cameo, in many families the power of the father is such that he inhibits the very interstices of his child's psyche, just as, according to Fanon, the black's psyche may be colonized by the white's. In such cases it is not the subject who speaks or thinks, but the other who has taken up occupation of the victim's internal world. Here uncritical thought will not simply be passive but will actively cling to a belief in the appearance of certain things. It actively refuses, rejects as perverse or crazy, any view which may contradict it.

To think critically one must therefore be able to use aggression to break through the limitations of one's own assumptions or to challenge the 'squatting rights' of the colonizer within one's own internal world. But there is a further element which follows quickly on the heels of this act of aggression, if the movement of thought is to be sustained: to be subversive one must be able to play. Take my own labour here as an example. I have started writing in an attempt to push my own understanding further. I have in front of me my own materials of production; mostly my own previous writings, notes on others' writings and my own subjectivity. All I can be sure of is that there is more to be known. That which waits to be known is, at present, beyond me. My fear is that I will examine these materials (which embody my present-day assumptions) but will be unable to put them to any further use. There will be no weakness or chink in the firm inertness they present to me. To move beyond them, to make use of them, I will have to be able to take hold of this *inert* structure, be prepared to abandon it, shake it, 'cut into it' and thereby deconstruct it. Only then will I be able to play and juggle within the ideas which this structure has frozen and in this way move towards a new synthesis. Milner (1955) notes that an act of destruction is often the prelude to play: before the child can, for instance, construct a new building she must be prepared to abandon the old. Once the materials have been freed, play, 'the manipulation of external phenomena in the service of the dream' (Winnicott, 1974), can begin.

All of this relates crucially to the question of my own human agency. If I cannot play with these materials they will demand my compliance (see the quotation from Winnicott at the beginning of this chapter). I will have to fit in with them, adapt to their whims and nuances. I will have become absorbed by my own assumptions, too closely identified with them. In other words, being too close to a set of ideas inhibits the exploration of new

possibilities (Robinson, 1984). On the other hand, being too distant pre-
vents any sensuous engagement with the material of production; there is
no dialogue or interplay, just meddling without passion. To really use ideas
one therefore has to maintain both an aggressive distance and an empathic
closeness (Khan, 1974).

'Aggression' seems to be an unfortunate word these days, largely because of its association with masculinity. Psychoanalysis is itself confused
about the proper role of aggression; sometimes associating it with the forces
of death, sometimes with the forces of life. Winnicott's (1975) analysis
begins with the foetus in the womb restlessly moving about, kicking at the
walls of the womb, sensing its environment through the opposition this
presents to its limbs. In other words, even at this stage of life the link
between aggression and exploration is clear. Not that the infant is being
aggressive in a hateful sense, for its activity is also an act of love, a form of
sensuous engagement with its environment. At this stage love and aggression are fused, intertwined to form a veritable life force. Note then how
both aggression and destructiveness are essential components of desire.
Without them there is no going beyond the given, no movement towards
'the new'.

The infant begins to understand its environment only by exploring the
limits, pushing at the boundaries. At first the boundaries will be physical –
the wall of the womb, the cot, the surface of the body of a parent who is
holding it – but later these boundaries will be largely psychical and social,
with rules being one of the most important forms. Testing the boundaries
of a situation therefore involves risk: there is always the possibility of
stubbing a toe or getting your fingers burnt.

Consider groups and organizations in this light: political groups,
community groups, welfare organizations. What stops a group from being
subversive is more often than not related to the constraints they impose
upon themselves, rather than the constraints which actually exist in the
external environment. In my experience we typically operate upon
situations in such a way as immediately to close off possibilities. We become
so absorbed by our own limiting assumptions that we quickly become
immersed in a business-like activity arranged within a disturbingly tight set
of parameters. Yet when a group breaks out of these parameters and
challenges its own assumptions, its power can be out of all proportion to
its size. Again in this light consider the power of the numerically
insignificant Bolshevik Party in making a popular revolution (Liebman,

1975). This is one thing reformism has never understood: the importance of the qualitative as well as the quantitative aspect of collective forms of struggle.

Just occasionally, perhaps twice only, have I been involved with groups which have taken off in this way. Once more, in my experience, the importance of an initial attitude of ruthlessness towards shared ideas and assumptions was crucial: a willingness to be disturbed, to challenge, even to abandon certain closely held beliefs in pursuit of the collective desire. And, once more, so was the element of play crucial but this time it was 'shared playing', a more difficult and developmentally more mature (Winnicott, 1974, pp. 44–61) operation to perform. As a group, people would throw ideas about, bounce ideas off each other, enrich each other's understanding through mutual offerings. Very often there would be a real element of excitement, partly sexual, as this 'playing with ideas' proceeded, out of which a new synthesis would emerge, very often encapsulated by a simple new idea: a kind of key, a device the potential power of which was clear to all present. This 'key' could assume any number of forms: a phrase which captured the 'new agenda' of an organization or movement, such as, 'economics as if people mattered'; a name for a cultural or political project (Ordine Nuovo); a new form of political or cultural analysis which hinged around a new concept or a previously existing concept which had been given new meaning, such as post-Fordism; a political strategy which seizes the imagination – 'can't pay, won't pay'. With this idea the group then could begin the process of collective objectification: the journey from the idea to its realization. Here is the real meaning of that enigmatic phrase 'the association of labour', a form of grouping or social bonding accomplished, not by terror (which appears to be the only form of bonding envisaged by Sartre) but through a kind of act of love. In my experience many organizations are held together by guilt and terror; many more are held together by bureaucracy and self-limiting assumptions. Just a few (and they are worth waiting for) are vehicles for collective desire.

To summarize this section: where do new ideas – and hence new forms of action which are capable of affecting unprecedented changes in the given – come from? Considered subjectively, they emerge from a process of aggressive abandonment, play and reconstruction. Each new configuration will, in turn, eventually become a constraint; each solution will, in time, become the problem. As Lenin said, truth lies in the continuation. But there is another, and perhaps more obvious, source to the imagination: the external world itself. But external reality will fuel our imagination only if we allow it to and it is to this that we now turn.

LEARNING FROM EXPERIENCE

[In] free imaginative drawing, the sight of a mark made on the
paper provokes new associations, the line as it were answers back
and functions as a very primitive type of external object.
Milner (1955, p. 92)

Milner is describing here the manner in which imaginative action may make use of experience and so move towards the realization of unforeseen possibilities. Whilst Milner uses examples from the arena of artistic production, I am convinced that all forms of production – political, material and mental – share a common form. We might then equally think of forms of political practice which produce unintended effects. When reality 'answers back' and surprises us, how do we learn from this in a way which enhances our practice?

Let us return to the act of drawing, for its simplicity enables us to distil elements of the process which might otherwise remain hidden. Through the simple act of leaving a mark on a piece of paper, something that was previously internal becomes outside us. In other words, some kind of transformation has occurred between our psychical and physical environment. There has been some kind of movement from the one to the other, the result of which is a physical mark – not any physical mark, but my human physical mark. Lest we overlook the fact, the mark on the piece of paper is in fact a complex human production; the young child will struggle for what must seem like an eternity before it can produce in this manner. Milner reminds us that even this most simple of human productions nevertheless has the capacity to speak to us in some way. We will develop our practice, however, only if we are prepared to listen to it, and we can listen to it only by being open to it, by being willing to be disturbed by it.

My experience is that most people involved in socialist politics have extreme difficulties in listening. In Britain we did not hear the class struggle subside with a return of a Labour Government in 1974. We did not hear the people's disenchantment with the Welfare State until it was already under attack and failing to gain popular support in its defence. We do not hear people's fears nor their aspirations, unless they assume a politically acceptable form. We listen only to what we wish to hear; it is a kind of political narcissism. Speaking of a narcissistic patient undergoing analysis, Winnicott describes a relationship between the narcissist and his experience which in many ways echoes our own relationship to political experiences:

> [The] subject never places the analyst outside and therefore can never do more than experience a kind of self-analysis, using the analyst as a projection of a part of the self. In terms of feeding, the patient, then, can feed only on the self and cannot use the breast for getting fat. The patient may even enjoy the analytic experience but will not fundamentally change. (1974, p. 107)

In other words, in such situations a dialogue of sorts exists but it is not one between self and other; it is between one part of the self and another part. The 'dialogue' is in fact a monologue: only the one story is being told by the one person, but with different voices. The 'objects' of this world are therefore invested with too much of our own subjectivity, and they therefore can give back to us only what has been put into them. That which is distinctively theirs remains unappreciated.

To return to an earlier example, imagine a young woman playing the piano. She is not reading from music but begins with a certain idea in mind; the idea refers to a brief melodic passage that she has hummed to herself and is now going to play. After some deliberation and several attempts she manages to put this idea to music. She now tries to extend the melody, to elaborate upon it. At this point she may encounter a difficulty we are familiar with: she begins to feel trapped within the melodic form she has so far managed to externalize. She endeavours to free herself from the structure in which she is becoming enmeshed; it might be that the trick is achieved when a new configuration is hit upon through some kind of accident (perhaps her finger slips). The key point is that she has allowed the piano to participate and in doing so has managed to emerge from the closure that the first melodic form was exerting. The result is neither something distinctly hers nor something that distinctly belongs to the piano, but something that acknowledges both the constraints and possibilities of both subject and object, a qualitative or multiplicative shift.

To learn from experience we must be able to engage in dialogue; we must allow the other to intrude into our subjective world. Only in this way can we receive something new, something not quite anticipated, and, if we allow ourselves to be affected by it, we may speak back to the agent of this intrusion in a way which demonstrates that it has been listened to.

'BEING' AND IMPROVISATION

We have already mentioned the role of play in the exploration of possibility, yet a moment's thought should suffice to indicate that there is something about the structure of play which marks it off from the forms of imaginative production existing within the terms set by Marx's model of the labour process.

In play, our desire carries us along and, although we produce new objects through it, the activity itself is objectless (without initial intent). Speaking of the great free jazz trumpeter Donald Cherry, Steve Lacy (1982) remarks: 'His way of going into the beyond and just taking off – to not worry about where you were coming from, but just to go – I wanted to be able to do that myself. It had something to do with my concepts of life and death and music.' The movement involved in this activity is much more akin to the movement we experience in a dream: there is no beginning, no end, no plan, no calculation. In dreams we surprise ourselves; we get carried away, sometimes against our better judgement. Here then our conscious intellectual faculties, our ego faculties, are suspended. This is the realm of improvisation, in art, music, politics, poetry and thought. Here one cannot 'force things'. It is a kind of gratuitous giving. This form of creativity is quite unlike purposeful and active forms of transformation. It is a 'letting go', a 'giving oneself up', an 'abandonment'.

An architect or a gardener can create something for which there is no precedent but this kind of creation is, in a sense, deliberate; indeed, it leaves nothing to chance: the gardener may lay and re-lay a lawn until she gets it 'just right', until reality 'fits' her conception. Although she must obey the laws of the material on which she works and approach her medium respectfully, there is nevertheless an element of inequality between herself and nature; she accepts the constraints offered by nature in order to transform it. She reaches out towards new possibilities by 'doing'. Now we must examine the other form of creative engagement based not so much on one's capacity 'to do' as 'to be'.

I have suggested that the second type corresponds to a kind of 'self-abandonment', to a 'giving oneself up'. It is important, however, not to conceive of this second type of creativity as a form of passivity.

The terms 'activity' and 'passivity' occur prominently within psychoanalysis. At times Freud equates them with the terms masculinity/femininity and on other occasions he argues that such an equation is invalid. In 'Instincts and their vicissitudes' (1915a), in particular, Freud considers activity and passivity as two basic forms (aims) of libidinal striving. It is useful to draw the parallel between satisfaction obtained by acting as an agent and 'activity', on the one hand, and satisfaction obtained by acting as an object and 'passivity', on the other. 'Activity', therefore, corresponds to desiring another; 'passivity' corresponds to 'being the object of another's desire'. Clearly, then, the term 'passivity' is somewhat deceptive, because the passive mode of gratification always involves a degree of personal action (you have to 'seduce' the other into desiring you). At times Freud implicitly takes account of this paradox and attempts to overcome it by arguing that all instinctual striving is active 'even when it has a passive aim in view' (1905). But here, as elsewhere, Freud explicitly makes an equation between 'activity' and 'masculinity', and therefore concludes that all instinctual striving is 'masculine'. Where then does 'femininity' fit in? One has to conclude that 'femininity' is (here and elsewhere) pushed out of his analytical work. He provides us with no adequate theorization of 'feminity'.

It is interesting to note therefore that D. W. Winnicott disposes of the terms activity and passivity completely, replacing them by three terms: 'Being', 'Doing' and 'Being done to'. In a radical departure from Freud, though one which is in fact a logical extension of Freud's suggestion that all libidinal striving is active/masculine, Winnicott argues that 'Being done to' corresponds to 'masculinity', as does 'Doing' itself. Thus, he argues, 'I associate impulse related to objects (also the passive voice of this) with the male element' (1974, p. 99).

The implications of this are far-reaching, for Winnicott is urging us to consider both activity and passivity as essentially 'masculine'. What then of 'femininity' in Winnicott's analysis? Winnicott answers us thus: 'The study of the pure distilled uncontaminated female element leads us to BEING, and this forms the only basis for self-discovery and a sense of existing. . . (1974, p. 97). As Winnicott himself is aware, this is equivalent to a fundamental reformulation of psychoanalytic theory:

> I have arrived at a position in which I say that object-relating in terms of *this pure female element has nothing to do with drive (or instinct)*. Object-relating backed by instinct belongs to the male element in the personality. . . The classical statement in regard to finding, using, oral eroticism, oral sadism, anal stages, etc arises out of a consideration of the pure male element. (1974, pp. 96–7).

Given the traditional usage of these terms, psychoanalysis and, by implication, Marxism is by and large an exposition of the 'masculine moment' of our subjectivity, of 'Doing' . Using Winnicott's terms, what is required is an equivalent theorization of the 'feminine moment' of 'Being': 'The male element *does* while the female element. . . is' (Winnicott, 1974, p. 95).

To return to the question of creativity, it is clear that classical psychoanalysis provides us with no conceptual space within which to locate the second type of creativity, other than the mystifying term 'passivity'. Using Winnicott's terminology, however, we may, if we so wish, consider this second type of creativity as a 'feminine creativity' and the first as an essentially 'masculine creativity'. However, there are dangers in using the terms 'masculine/feminine' to denote psychological dispositions, so I will simply assert that the first type corresponds to the sphere of Doing, the second to the sphere of Being. What does this enable us to say about creators of the second type, the improvisers? First, that the artist or musician who creates spontaneously is not so much 'acting upon' the canvas or piano as she is 'Being-by-virtue-of-the-canvas/piano'. The question is not so much one of what the pianist does; rather, it is a question of what the pianist at that moment 'is'. When asked if, during the creative act, his mind went blank, Steve Lacy replies:

> Not exactly a blank – more like a blink. You try and stay out of the way. You try and not lose touch with the music, and let the thing happen. It's not you that does it – it's IT that wants to be done. . . It can only go one way, and it's not you who decides, it's IT. (1982)

When I am sad, I can talk to another of this sadness but my words can never fully capture the feeling. It is difficult to 'be sad' whilst speaking; words have habit of carrying us away from such things rather than leading us to them. Occasionally, by finding the right word or turn of phrase, my conversation will draw the other's attention to this sadness. The words act as signs directing the other's gaze, but because they are signs they exist at one remove from the sadness itself; the words themselves are 'empty'. However, just occasionally, rather than talking of my sadness I may talk sadly. I may use 'sad words', words which do not just refer to something some way off but words which are full of the sadness itself. This is a form of poetry: the achievement of the poet is to write a 'sad poem' rather than a poem which is about sadness. This kind of creativity is an expression of the person's Being. Whilst, as in the case of poetry, words may be used as the medium of production, the product itself is essentially pre-verbal, at the level of mood, of feeling and of passion, modes of experience which precede and provide the necessary conditions for the development of language in later infancy. As Winnicott exclaims in a statement which resembles a manifesto at the end of his fascinating essay, 'After Being – Doing and Being Done to. But first, Being' (1974, p. 99).

BEYOND MARX AND FREUD

For the time being, at least, we live in a 'man's world'. It should come as no surprise therefore to find that neither the Marxism of Marx nor the psycho-analysis of Freud has anything of substance to say about the question of Being. Theirs are philosophies of Doing and its passive voice. One can search in vain but they have little to tell us about play, empathy, intuition or improvisation. For a full understanding of human powers, therefore, we must go beyond Marx and Freud. Psychoanalysis itself is now shifting its focus to the pre-oedipal, to the pre-linguistic stage of infancy in which the basic struggle of the infant relates to its concern to establish a secure sense of Being. I wonder if there are similar currents at work in Marxism which might bring a similar shift in focus, so that the philosophy of doing might be complemented by a philosophy of being?

The problem of Being and the struggle 'to be' is the basis of the theory of the psychoses. Without a secure sense of his own Being, 'the man of action' engages in a kind of frenzied thrashing. Life takes on a compulsive character. Male narcissism saturates almost every tissue of the society in which we live; a form of madness which passes itself off as normalcy. The stronger our desire for recognition the more we reveal our essential

—

insufficiency. If we are strangers to ourselves what hope is there that others might recognize us?

NOTES

1 *A note on the psychoanalytic 'object'*: The concept of the 'object' and 'object relations' has been central to the development of psychoanalysis since Freud. One hears, for example, of 'the self engaged in a parasitic relationship with its objects' or of a self for whom the passage from object-relating to object-usage has only just been precariously established. The analysis provided by Laplanche and Pontalis (1973) of such terms as 'cathexis', 'object' and 'object relationship' shows that their exact status and meaning within psychoanalysis are not unambiguous.

   In this book I use the term 'object' in what I believe is its main psychoanalytic sense, as 'the idea' one has of something – which may be animate or inanimate, internal or external – to which one is emotionally connected. Thus 'the object' is essentially 'the idea' one forms about one's father, garden, car or television, one's body or a part of one's body, a particular group (such as Jews); indeed, any such things which have acquired specific conscious or unconscious personal meaning.

   The emotional cathexis of 'the idea' may be positive, negative or it may assume the form of an anti-cathexis. In the latter instance an apparent absence of concern or interest in the object masks a relationship which is dangerously charged. Clearly, psychoanalytic objects are 'psychical objects' not 'physical objects'; in other words they are objects full of conscious and unconscious meaning. The nature of the interpenetration of the psychical and the physical has belatedly become an issue of real concern within contemporary psychoanalysis; it should also be of equal concern to any theory of social action. Within psychoanalysis it leads us to ask various questions. How do actual properties of the object inform the character of the psychical object (in other words, how does the behaviour of the real mother influence the kind of psychical object she comes to represent for her daughter)? How do one's psychical objects come to influence the behaviour and character of the actual object (that is, if one repeatedly projects highly noxious psychical material onto another in such a covert way that they have no means of processing it, what might this do to their health)? The unconscious idea I might have of my word processor is of a machine which attacks my capacity for linking different thoughts; I may share with others an idea of my political party as an object of purification and cold love; my musical instrument may contain some of the character of a sexual organ. In each case the way in which I take action in the physical world is affected by the character of my 'psychical object world'. Now I am aware that to the casual reader these examples may seem 'far-fetched'. I, on the other hand, regard them as perfectly 'normal' phenomena – the madness of normality. Incredulous readers are encouraged to suspend disbelief so that they might engage in some kind of dialogue with this book.

2 *Fantasy and Phantasy.* Throughout this book I have endeavoured to sustain the vital distinction psychoanalysis makes between fantasy and phantasy. 'Fantasy' refers to the more familiar sense of a mental activity which is conscious and akin to day-dreaming. The concept of 'phantasy', introduced by Melanie Klein into contemporary psychoanalysis, refers to a quite different mental activity: one which is almost entirely unconscious.

3

The Culture of Uncertainty

The crisis consists precisely in the fact that the old is dying and the new cannot be born; in this interregnum a great variety of morbid symptoms appear. . . The death of the old ideologies takes the form of scepticism with regards to all theories and general formulae. . . and to a form of politics which is not simply realistic in fact (this is always the case) but which is cynical in its immediate manifestation.

Antonio Gramsci, *The Prison Notebooks,* 1977, p. 246

The recurrent configuration is of an explosive force within a restraining framework.

Wilfred Bion, *Attention and Interpretation,* 1970, p. 79

The great waves of capitalist development, sometimes referred to as Kondratiev waves, which have punctuated the last 200 years of world history have resulted in the continuous construction, destruction and reconstruction of the world we live in. Each new wave of development amounts to a qualitatively distinct form of capitalist society. To compare the form of the industrial corporation, the family or the state during the classical period of imperialism at the beginning of the twentieth century with the new forms which developed after the Second World War is to compare two sets of quite distinct phenomena. We cannot predict what new forms will emerge if capitalism manages to come through its present profound crisis to a new wave of development. We can, however, agree with Carlotta Peres (1983) that the social and institutional innovations which facilitated the post-war boom constitute 'a list of obsolete mechanisms as regards the effective institutions required to unleash the upswing of the fifth Kondratiev based on microelectronics' (p. 371). The Keynesian Welfare State, the big mass-production companies, monopoly capitalism, neo-colonialism, these and many other institutional arrangements which were central to the development of the post-war boom now confront us as problems and obstacles rather than solutions.

If we can agree that successive mutations in the form of capitalism have profound effects upon our ways of life then a history of cultural forms tracing the interrelationship between waves of capitalist development and trends within literature, art, philosophy and politics would seem to be possible; indeed over sixty years ago Trotsky (1923) speculated upon this very possibility.

My impression is that such an analysis has yet to be undertaken. What I would like to examine here is something slightly different. Rather than focus upon cultural discontinuities, I would like to consider the possibility of cultural continuity or, more accurately, recursivity within culture. The observation I would share is this: irrespective of the different embryonic social forms that were incubating within them, each successive 'great recession' has etched a similar pattern upon the grain of collective human sentiment. In other words, there have been repeated themes in the way in which culture has performed its working through of economic and social crisis. To this extent one can speak of recurring 'cultures of uncertainty' marked by a number of essential ideas, emotions and orientations bound up with a complex we might usefully describe as being one of failed dependency. It is to an exploration of such sentiments that I would now like to turn.

To live through a deep-seated crisis within capitalist society is to participate in a period of uncertainty where all existing answers have ceased to serve. We are used to speaking of 'the economic crisis' but the sense of crisis I am reaching for goes beyond this. All of our certainties – economic, moral, political and aesthetic – are presently shaken. Moreover, not only do the old solutions no longer work. Worse than this, they now seem positively to contribute to the straits we find ourselves in. For those who, in the past, always considered themselves to be 'part of the solution' this is perplexing indeed.

The situation we are in affects each one of us personally and deeply. I say this in the full realization that some will disagree. The 'fundamentalist Left' will argue that there is indeed a crisis 'out there', in society, but it is not one that affects them. They will argue that objectively things are ripe for change, the problem is in the 'subjective factor', the absence of a political party capable of bringing about a revolutionary transformation. Closer inspection, however, reveals that this is not a prescient piece of self-criticism. No, the party exists, the problem is that the people won't come to it! The fact that this so-called 'crisis of the subjective factor'[1] appears to have existed since the destruction of revolutionary Marxism by fascism and Stalinism fifty years ago does not appear to have shaken their belief that the problem lies with the people (and their present leaders) and not with the party. I think this kind of attitude is clearly 'part of the problem' we now face. It is indicative of a process of splitting 'out there' from 'in here', the 'objective' from the 'subjective', external from internal.

The truth, that we no longer have answers, hurts. And the pain is greatest for those who have striven the most conscientiously to use a system of thought as an instrument for turning a barren existence into one rich with meaning. On the other hand, where ideas are clung to as a badge of faith, as a way of erasing the nagging search for understanding, no uncertainty will be felt. If crises are always, potentially, turning points – for economy, culture and politics – then the problem for Marxism has been its traditional reluctance to turn. To this extent it has taken on the form of a 'restraining framework', a form of consolation to be adhered to in face of the explosive force of truth. But the more we cling, the more we betray our own deep anxiety. So we see that the crisis does affect us all internally, the difference being that some cannot contain this anxiety and work on it but adhere all the more desperately to that which provided comfort in the past.

This is the dilemma at the heart of truth-seeking. Our language betrays our predicament. As Balint (1959) noted, when we speak of 'understanding', we speak in terms of 'grasping' something. The best we can ever hope for is to have a grip on things which is 'good enough'; one that is adequate to the tasks facing us but never complete or perfect. For the problem soon becomes one of relaxing our grip sufficiently for the journey of truth to begin again. This then is the problem of depressive anxiety, of 'letting go' and 'leaving behind' sufficiently for development to proceed whilst holding on to the feeling that what had been arrived at was basically good and valuable. Failure to adopt this depressive state of mind forces us to cling rigidly to a framework which no longer guides but traps; and the more the force of truth threatens to explode this understanding, the more desperately we idealize it.

However, my impression is that the resurgence of fundamentalism is not the main problem we on the Left face at the moment. There has been a far more striking development than this, noticeable particularly within what were once 'progressive' sections of the intelligentsia. I would link it to a failure to maintain the depressive position in the context of failed dependency; as a result old attachments cannot be left with any dignity, they must be attacked and spoiled, for only in that way can their grip be relinquished. The perceived failure of existing totalizing systems such as psychoanalysis and Marxism leads to an attack upon the idea that the construction of organizing systems of thought is possible, that is, upon the possibility of what Bion would call 'the selected fact'.[2]

The basis for such an attack lies in the crisis of the very idea of progress. This in itself is not unique. As Gramsci's comments suggest, the idea of progress was no less subject to doubt in the 1920s than it is today. Of course, since then man has proved capable of acts of cold savagery and impersonal destruction which to us seem unprecedented. How can one be optimistic with this kind of legacy? Yet reality itself, even the most stark and horrific, never leaves a simple imprint upon consciousness. The bomb, the camps, the liquidation of the Soviet peasantry and opposition, all of these things had occurred by the 1950s and 1960s, yet hardly for a moment did they dent our confidence in the idea that 'we'd never had it so good'. Though I fear that to some this may sound crude, periods of economic development and economic crisis do produce contrasting, popular, barely conscious sentiments. I would not wish to call them optimism and pessimism, for I feel these describe very particular and vital human attitudes that I will investigate later. Rather, I suggest we use the term 'contentment', the attitude of the infant feeding at the bountiful breast – which, as we know, is a temporary illusion – to describe those sentiments bound up with economic development, and 'resentment' to describe the sentiments evoked by crisis. Such sentiments, then, mediate our perception of reality, its triumphs and its catastrophes. I could not, at this moment, give much more meaning to these two collective sentiments. Suffice it to say that contentment would appear to carry with it a strong element of what one might call 'omniscient complacency' whereas 'resentment' carries with it much irritability, the kind of irritability experienced when one is abruptly ejected from a state of grace.

Let us probe a little deeper into this disbelief in progress, for allthough at one level it concerns itself with the real world problems of unemployment or warfare, at another level it reveals quite primitive and catastrophist assumptions. Consider the following extracts. The first comes from Oswald Spengler's (1926) work *The Decline of the West,* which was published just after the end of the First World War, at the beginning of the last great world recession. Then come two extracts from contemporary writers speaking on the issue of 'post-modernism'.

First Spengler:

> We are civilized people; we have to reckon with the hard cold facts of *late* life, to which the parallel is to be found not in Pericles's Athens but in Caesar's Rome. Of great painting or great music there can no longer be, for Western people, any question. Their architectural possibilities have been exhausted these hundred years. Only *extensive* possibilities are left to them. . . It has been the convention hitherto to admit to no limits of any sort in these matters. . . now, nobody but a pure romantic would take this way out. What are we to think of the individual who, standing before an *exhausted* quarry, would rather be told that a new vein will be struck tomorrow. . . than be shown a rich and virgin clay-bed near by? (1926, p. 40; my emphases)

Note here the references to ancient Rome, the cold and weary realism and its antipathy to romanticism, but above all savour the repeated reference to 'exhaustion'. Now to Jameson:

> there is another sense in which the writers and artists of the present day will no longer be able to invent new styles and worlds – they've already been invented; only a limited number of combinations are possible; the most unique ones have been thought of already. . . all that is left is to imitate dead styles. (1983, p. 115)

And to Baudrillard:

> space is so saturated, the pressure so great from all who want to make themselves heard. . . (1983, p. 132)

We see then how the crisis in the idea of progress recurrently evokes the idea of the end of human development – all forms, all ideas, all aesthetics, all moralities have been exhausted. It is the fantasy of an exhausted breast with nothing left to give and, at this deeper level, the abandonment of hope. Here we have the intellectual's nightmare, that the thing he or she has been labouring over for months or years is also about to be produced by someone else. The intelligentsia's world has become peopled by doppelgängers, the possibility of transcendence has gone. No one can any longer leave their mark. There are no more Nietzsches, Freuds, Joyces or, for that matter, Presleys. The seam has been exhausted. An army of cultural miners fight over scraps and flotsam left by predecessors who still had a real job to do.

The end of thought invokes an era of intellectual petty commodity production in which we scrape a living like the street boys once did in Saigon, selling single cigarettes to passers-by. Enter an era of anti-thought in which the intelligentsia's only role is to pour scorn on those misguided fools who still speak of commitment. . . 'really, darling, how naive, it's all been tried before!'

This is not pessimism, but hatred and despair. Having been caught once in an embrace with something which was good but then failed, one resolves firmly never to be caught again. The only future for culture lies in 'debunking' and pastiche, either the merciless stripping bare of tired systems or a coprophilic fiddling with, and agglomeration of, cultural antiques. This is a pre-depressive attitude, one without the grace or courage to acknowledge past dependencies. This is not scepticism but cynicism, a crucial difference as we shall see.

Some describe this as 'going relativist' (D'Amico, 1986). But if 'anything' goes this is not the sentiment of the 1960s (for whom today's relativists have the utmost scorn). In the 1960s this was emancipation from the rule of the father, from the law of restraint and unquestioning 'responsibility'. For the relativists of the 1980s, those who once opened our prison gates (Freud, Marcuse, Laing, Marx, Luxemburg, Mao) are the real authority from whom they now promise liberation. Not surprisingly the more they cry, 'Anything goes,' the more that others cling to their systems, to their consolations. A cultural nihilism feeds off and reproduces a set of petrified totalities. More importantly, each of these orientations emerges from a fundamental incapacity to bear frustration. Thus cynicism, despite its stylish garb, and fundamentalism share the same emotionally primitive foundation.

Both orientations are forms of thoughtlessness, that is, they are primarily positions from which meaning is attacked rather than nurtured. The difference, however, is this: the fundamentalist considers an event and, refusing to be fooled by appearances, reads into it only what he has evacuated from his own constipated mental system. No dialogue occurs; events provide no food for thought; such systems can only feed off their own (waste) products (Robinson, 1984). The cynic, on the other hand, refuses to be fooled by the idea that there is any depth to events at all. There is nothing more to behold than meets the eye; it is as if 'general laws were only meant for the stupid' (Sloterdijk, 1984). Whereas the one sees some meaning (if only the meaning of its own reflection), the other refuses the idea of meaning altogether. Bion calls this latter 'anti-thought', something more radically pathological than simple thoughtlessness

> it shows itself as a superior object asserting its superiority by finding fault with everything. The most important characteristic is its hatred of any new development. . . as if the new development were a rival to be destroyed. The emergence therefore of any tendency to search for the truth, to establish contact with reality and in short be scientific in no matter how rudimentary a fashion is met by destructive attacks on the tendency and the reassertion of the 'moral' superiority. (Bion, 1962, p. 98)

So, whereas fundamentalism is a form of ideological secondary narcissism (scientific but in the most primitive fashion) cynicism's only purpose lies in the collection of meaningful elements 'so that these elements can be stripped of their meaning and only the worthless residue retained. . . denudation not abstraction is the end product' (Bion, 1962, pp. 98–9). This, I fear, is where Lyotard's (1984) 'pragmatics of language particles' takes us. As such, far from constituting any kind of critique of the society of the fragmentary image, post-modernism stands as its champion and exemplar. The task of culture, to go beneath the surface of things, is abandoned for the celebration of surface-itiality (to borrow from this fashionable form of expression). We are by now used to the way in which the misfortune of some becomes 'high fashion' for others; we can only gasp when this is done to the ultimate nightmare of psychosis.

So far I have used a restricted sense of terms like 'culture' and 'intelligentsia' as if in some way this referred to a class of opinion-leaders. It is important to extend this sense to one that includes the general category of intellectual labourers in our society; in other words, to those privileged enough to have a training and education to be in a position to know better. For my perception is that such cynicism is becoming a popular sentiment within this social layer. One encounters it for instance in many varieties of public servant – educators, planners, accountants – and in general in 'the professional classes'. I have found the writing of Peter Sloterdijk (1984) provocative in this context.

He speaks of cynicism no longer being an individual attribute, more a diffuse cultural phenomenon. For the educated, cynicism is the price to be paid for survival during a recession in which justice appears to have been defeated. Sloterdijk calls this an accommodation which knows about itself, one in which 'we see a detached negativity which scarcely allows itself any hope, at most a little irony and self-pity' (p. 194). He uses the term 'enlightened false consciousness' to describe an inward-looking fatalism which is nevertheless subliminally aware of its own retreat. It is an attitude which accepts the rewards of the system through a little self-parody. For example, one jokingly speaks of 'selling out' when personally laying out 'thousands' on a new car. The witticism here is meant to signal one's detachment from the career planning, home developing, consumption-orientated lifestyle that one's behaviour might otherwise suggest. It is not easy for 'progressives' to become 'normals' without much self-conscious-ness. In place of a broad moral and historical perspective life becomes filled with little projects – word processors to be bought and mastered, research in some urgent (but localized) social problem, a shift into freelance work and out of the oppressiveness of public institutions. These developments can be rationalized as contributing to some grander, longer-term transfor-mative goal. But all the time, in the background, other thoughts keep breaking in, fuelling this uneasy humour.

Because of our background we should know better and, indeed, a part of us does know better. A small, split-off part knows that we have become complicit in a broader sentiment of hopelessness through which the force-fulness of our enemies has been allowed to assume the majesty of fate. We know that late-twentieth-century politics is all about dancing on the edge, and that if the odds are not quite against us surviving, then what of our children and our children's children? We know of the ruination of the Amazon basin and its peoples. We know that others starve while we eat, and in style. We know of the results of the application of science to torture so that victims cannot prematurely die. We have heard that arms are necessary to keep the peace; greed to feed the hungry; secrecy to preserve freedom. We know these and a thousand other things, being educated types, but it no longer arouses our passion except perhaps when in moments of impotent fury we fantasize acts of political murder. 'To be intelligent and to perform one's work in spite of it, that is the unhappy consciousness in its modernized form' (Sloterdijk, 1984, p. 194). One is reminded of Sartre's concept of 'bad faith'.

Yet we also know that others do fight, do continue to commit themselves to what seems like an unequal struggle. However, the problem for a renewed politics today is how to be hopeful without recourse to faith. The cynic would say that 'to hope' in these times is to find salvation in calculated naivety; better not to kid ourselves again than embark upon another self-deceiving commitment. Well, in times like these, when it seems that defeat gets piled upon defeat, at least the cynic doen't run the risk of being proved wrong yet again. But of course this is the hidden basis of the cynic's own consolation. By never putting oneself in a position where one has to take sides, let alone take action on the basis of such judgements, one can retain what Bion called an attitude of 'moral superiority'.

As Meltzer *et al.* note (1975, p. 241) political action can only ever proceed from an imperfect basis. Effective action is always based upon an incomplete understanding. If one were to wait until one had really studied a situation; was convinced that the evidence available really did point to certain conclusions; had consciously striven to explore and entertain the opposite point of view before rejecting it; if one did all those things, then one would never take action until it was too late. In political as well as group and therapeutic settings, the issue of 'timing' is essential – an 'intervention' is a particular form of action in which the issue of 'when' is as important as 'what'. Moreover, there is but a short step from a 'questioning consciousness' to a fear of learning from experience. To say that all action necessarily proceeds from an uncertain basis means that in taking action we must live with the fear of an experience which cannot be anticipated. This makes it difficult for thoughtful people to become active (I'm sure many of them end up being analysts or psychotherapists where a sustained capacity to be 'in doubt and uncertainty' is perceived as the only helpful attitude); as difficult indeed as it is for active people to become thoughtful. How to combine decisiveness with thoughtfulness, a 'visionary consciousness' with a 'questioning consciousness', are the issues we must resolve.

Meltzer's argument is that action can take place only on the basis of a splitting process. To act decisively one must have some sense of being right. Given that there are no absolute truths we can be sure of, we have to suspend doubt temporarily in order to act upon what seems like the most justified position. Of course, we may have backed the wrong horse, but in taking action we have to assume that we are right, the other wrong. Thus good is on our side; the bad on theirs. A certain idealization and projection are inevitable but, as we know, such processes can equally be in the service of development as of regression. The problem then is how to act decisively, with the passion that stems from feeling right and good, yet preserve the capacity to be proved wrong. For this is what distinguishes an intervention from an 'act of faith', and a starting point must be the consciousness of risk. To know risk is to know that one might be wrong but to act in spite of this. It is, then, to toy in public with the possibility of one's moral and intellectual imperfection; it is to hand over one's narcissism as if it were a hostage voluntarily given to an opposing position. An intervention is, to use Balint's (1959) formulation, inherently philobatic,[3] a step into the unknown which may result in one being brought roughly down to earth.

To know risk is to realize the necessity of toleration. To know that one might be wrong is to know that one has no monopoly on the truth. On the other hand, we know that a key characteristic of fundamentalism is its intolerance. In this way it reveals the regressive and paranoid foundation of its splitting between right and wrong. It is a basically ungenerous attitude where others are refused 'the benefit of the doubt'. There are no grey areas, the fissure between the ideal and the rotten is complete. As Meltzer *et al.* (1978, p. 105) note, this is the Old Testament attitude of 'Those who are not with me must be against me'. It is an attitude which assumes the worst in others; unlike the contrary New Testament attitude which presumes that 'Those who are not against me must be with me'. Within the latter the will is still optimistic; it is an optimism based on a benign view of human and group development, of people's capacity to struggle through to find answers which, even if not identical with one's own, are certainly no less just and truthful.

In writing these passages I am trying to develop my own understanding of Gramsci's phrase 'pessimism of the intellect, optimism of the will', a phrase which has proved extremely irritating to some recent commentators on the Left like Ralph Miliband (1985) but which I have always found profoundly pleasing. 'Pessimism of the intellect' has been the most easy to comprehend – then as now the problem was to develop forms of political practice which were not reliant upon a background teleology; to develop a Marxism which could face reality without crutches. But how can we concretely understand something which seems so voluntaristic as 'optimism of the will'? I feel Gramsci provides a clue when elsewhere in *The Prison Notebooks* he talks about the relationship between action and passion.   .

I feel that there may exist two paths towards truth. For Bion the appearance of truth is akin to the birth of meaning – an 'immaculate conception'; though in this case one with a proper parentage. We know the centrality of Keats's phrase 'when a man is capable of being in doubt and uncertainty without irritable reaching after fact or reason' to Bion's sense of the truth-seeker. This is a quietistic path, equivalent to a period of confinement in which eros achieves its task of synthesis, binding and bringing together fragments of previous understandings into a new whole.

But there is another path, the active one of *experimental action.* Here reality is not a 'given' to be deciphered but a process of becoming to be engaged with. For Gramsci this is the difference between a 'political scientist' and a 'politician'. In his essay, 'The modern prince', Gramsci notes 'the political scientist has to keep within the bounds of effective reality in so far as he is merely a scientist. But Machiavelli is not merely a scientist: he is a *partisan,* a man of powerful passions, an active politician, who wishes to create a new balance of forces. . .' (1977, p. 172). Whereas the former understands reality, the latter creates it. Who is closer to the truth?

And if we think on this, is not the psychoanalyst partisan? Does he or she not 'take sides' with the forces of life? Do we not hear of the 'analytical intervention', of the importance of 'timing'? I wonder then if Bion has told us just one side of the story; the side with the 'purer' form. For, although the other side is undoubtedly messy, there seems little point in understanding a patient or group only after the encounter has ceased. No, we have to grasp at fragments and live with the risk this necessarily involves.

Perhaps the difference between the political and the analytical partisan lies in the nature of their passion. For, as Gramsci notes, the politician bases passion on a sense of 'what ought to be'. But this is not necessarily a regressive yearning for an idealized system. As he notes, 'the attribute "utopian" does not apply to political will in general, but to specific wills which are incapable of relating means to an end and hence are not even wills, but idle whims, dreams, longings etc.' (1977, p. 175).

This is faith, 'nothing other than the clothing worn by real and active will when in a weak position' (p. 337); it is not passion. This passion is a fusion of anger and love. It is an anger which comes from 'one's own better knowledge' harnessed constructively; not split off in murderous fantasy, to fuel an attention which can be directed violently towards the present, 'that pathological itch to scratch surfaces for concealed depths' (Eagleton, 1985, p. 70). This is what Gramsci means by 'pessimism of the intelligence'. But it is a love also, a love based upon a deep identification with a benign object; not perfect, but 'good enough' to keep alive an inner conviction that things can be different, indeed that people have in them the capacity to make a difference. This then is what perhaps both Gramsci and Winnicott in their different ways meant by 'optimism': the experience of hope in object relating.

NOTES

1 The use of the terms 'subjective' and 'objective' factors has been a characteristic of Leninist and Trotskyist thought since the formation of the Third International in 1919. The significance of these concepts to the revolutionary movement lay in their intimate connection with a world view which assumed that European capitalism was 'objectively' disintegrating under the weight of its own contradictions and hence the revolutionary transformation was not only immanent but also imminent. The only factor missing was the revolutionary party, that is, the 'subjective' factor. The crude and simple counterposition of these two terms can be criticized in many ways – for instance, the prolonged absence of a revolutionary party surely in itself constitutes an element of the 'objective factor'. Moreover, in orthodox style 'the subjective' is made equivalent to 'the party' as if only the latter were capable of bringing about a change in the given.

2 Bion uses the term 'selected fact' to refer to a particular form of thought which has the property of giving organization to incoherent and fragmented experience. It is a property which enables the subject to emerge from a state in which psychotic anxiety, that is, persecution by doubt and the chaos of experience, predominates (Bion, 1962).

3 In *Thrills and Regressions* Balint develops a theorization of two essentially contrasting object-relational configurations resembling Fairbairn's notion of the phobic and counter-phobic orientations. For Balint the ocnophile is one who finds excitement and security by staying close to objects of desire. The philobat (based upon the Greek word for acrobat), on the other hand, derives excitement and security from inhabiting the

wide open spaces between objects (though the philobat may need objects, typically instruments of one kind or another, to maintain his or her balance).

4

'The Labour of Love' and 'A Primary Social Medium': Two Problematics in Contemporary Psychoanalysis

Thе idea that psychoanalysis somehow constitutes a coherent and monolithic totalizing system is so far removed from the reality of the history of this movement – a movement which at times could even have taught the revolutionary Left a thing or two about factionalism – that one sometimes wonders whose interests the perpetuation of this myth has served. Nevertheless, despite this plurality of traditions and languages, some key common concerns do run throughout psychoanalysis. Perhaps *the* most essential of these hinges upon the question of subjectivity and, particularly, how this subjectivity emerges from an original nature which is corporeal and physical. For, like it or not, this is the psychoanalytic starting point: that we come into this world and depart from it by virtue of our corporeality. This is not to say that 'biology is destiny'; rather, it is simply to state that like any other natural phenomenon we have some 'grain' which gives shape to the range of forms that this human material of ours can acquire.

The idea that human existence is marked by some kind of 'existential contradiction' seems to be returning to modern social theory; indeed, it is particularly striking in the work of Anthony Giddens. Yet, as I have suggested, this has always been at the heart of psychoanalysis. The American object-relations analyst Harold Searles put the question succinctly. How is it possible to be 'a part of nature and yet apart from all the rest of non-human nature?' (1960, p. 104). How do we live this contradiction throughout our own individual development? How, in this sense, does phylogeny reproduce ontogeny?

For many years, despite the efforts of occasional detractors like Federn, Fenichel and Reich, psychoanalysis sought to explore this contradiction from a position in which misrecognition was the only possibility. The problem was that psychoanalysis approached its task and erected its system on just two legs – physical and psychical reality – where three were needed. The third, social reality, was missing or, if present, turned out upon analysis to be a chimera; a complex externalization of an essential individual psychology.

Fortunately over the last forty years psychoanalysis has slowly discovered its missing term and the work of the object-relations theorists Donald Winnicott and Michael Balint and Wilfred Bion's singular trajectory from his Kleinian base has been seminal here. It seems to me that this work suggests two fundamental problematics within human development, each of which has vital relevance for socialist thought. To Winnicott and Balint I feel we owe the idea of what I can only describe as a 'primary social medium'; a medium which is essentially social but with an experienced texture which is physical in its fluidity and, indeed, which originates from a physical prototype. To Bion I feel we owe the idea of the first human labour process which, I argue later, is no more than 'the labour of love'; the first work of transformation without which we could never emerge from our physical universe, that is, from our original nature.

At many points I feel that these two problematics do overlap, the writers using more or less the same language to describe the same phenomenon; at other points they are clearly separate and irreducible to one another. Whilst they each plough the same field, the configurations they make are only occasionally identical.

Let me begin by elaborating upon the idea of a primary social medium. What first drew my attention to the possibility of such a phenomenon was my experience as a consultant within unstructured groups. There is something very primitive about such groups, which is presumably why psycho-analysis has been fascinated with them for so long.[1] They are primitive not least because those 'running' such groups have taken pains to strip them bare. The group has no objective which can be understood in terms of the ordinary meaning of 'a task to busy oneself with'; there appear to be no rules or precedents. There are no distractions provided to kill time with. There are no props, save the chairs that participants sit upon; there are none of civilization's little comforts. Participants speak of being 'set adrift', of having the experience of being 'all at sea'. When participants attempt to share an experience with the groups they find their words quickly 'sink without trace'. Others speak of the difficulty of 'floating an idea' about what the group might do. Indeed, some ideas do float for a while but, the more people cling to them the more quickly they 'go under'. As consultant, I am often tempted to say, 'Only those afraid of sinking need fear water.' It is as if one is witness to the aftermath of a shipwreck – survivors drift about clinging to bits of wreckage, some thrash about, causing a stir. It strikes me that the first task of such a group, one which precedes the possibility of any work being performed, is to realize that the medium in which it finds itself suddenly immersed will support it if it lets it. Discovering the nature of this medium is equivalent to establishing intersubjectivity. I am always re-minded of Bion's remark at the opening of 'Group dynamics' in this context: 'The adult must establish contact with the emotional life of the group in which he lives; this task would appear to be as formidable to the adult as the relationship with the breast appears to be to the infant' (1961, pp. 141–2).

Regarding the phrase 'establishing contact' we might note in passing how much mystery and complexity are concealed behind this simple facade. I might also add that this process of establishing contact arouses ambivalent feelings: the more some participants learn to trust the medium the more frenziedly others thrash around in it; the more some shout, 'Come on in, the water's lovely,' the more others grow to hate them.

Leaving the group for a moment, we might also note how, in our everyday language, we speak of 'immersing ourselves in a subject' or of being 'anchorless' or 'rudderless'. Think also of the connotations of 'free floating attention', as used within psychoanalysis to describe the proper analytic orientation. All such evidence from everyday language suggests the existence of some medium which is at the heart of our intersubjectivity. The phrase 'drowning not waving' sharply brings us in touch with another essential human experience, that of 'breakdown'. Interestingly, both Klei-nian and object-relations analysts consistently use the metaphor of 'drown-ing' or 'falling' to get at the phenomenology of emotional breakdown. As we shall see later, Bion coins the phrase 'catastrophic anxiety' to describe this experience. It is, in many senses, the most terrifying of all human experiences. Indeed, it is the most primary of all anxieties, as it refers to the fantasy of psychical death itself.

How, then, can we approach an understanding of this primary social medium? I would argue that without the discovery of this medium and the development of the capacity to trust oneself to it, it is impossible for the infant to emerge properly into a human universe. As humanly natural beings, we are transformative beings, that is, we are of nature and yet set apart from nature. This is our destiny, like it or not. Our being 'set apart from' is the necessary condition for our being transformative. Without this distance from nature, from others and from ourselves, we cannot become rational beings nor can we use physical or human 'objects' according to our purposes, nor can there be any self-consciousness or species conscious-ness. But, whilst to the adult observer the newly born baby is already 'set apart' from the mother who delivered it into this world, the phenomenolo-gical world of the infant knows of no such distinctions: there is no 'me' and 'not me'; no 'inside' and no 'outside'. This is what object-relations theory means by an original state of undifferentiatedness.

Freud attempted to grasp this phenomenon but did so from a position whereby the person was essentially constituted monadically (Bercherie, 1986). His theory of primary narcissism assumes the individual as an island – the other is absent; as a consequence, narcissism is construed endogen-ously and not as an intersubjective phenomenon. Later, as his own work becomes more properly object-relational, Freud touches upon this same phenomenon but through the idea of 'primary identification' which he suggests is the earliest expression of an emotional tie with another person' (1921). Let us note the distinction here, one that Freud does not always make, between identification as the very first form of relating and those secondary identifications based around the introjection of desired and/or terrifying others. At the stage of primary identification there are 'no others' phenomenologically speaking; there is no duality of terms let alone 'the third'. The infant's world is undifferentiated, but from the very beginning it is involved in relationship to others. Indeed, these are the most important relationships of its life, truly life-or-death relationships, although ones it is quite unaware of.

Through his notion of 'primary identification', Freud was approaching the idea that from the outset the infant lives by virtue of being in relationship to another. Extending the logic of this, Winnicott argues that at first 'the individual' is not the unit, 'as perceived from outside the unit is an environ-ment-individual set-up' (1952, p. 221).

There is a certain 'atomism' that much of psychoanalysis unwittingly borrowed from the prevailing scientific culture in which it emerged. This causes it to speak of the infant's 'first object' when in reality at first no objects exist. So where analysts such as Grotstein (1985) try to get at the phenom-enology of the beginnings of human life by using phrases such as 'the background object of primary identification' to refer to the status of the parental figures, our attention should more properly be focused upon the sense of 'the background' as being 'non-object'. I have often found Balint helpful here. He illustrates how the foetal environment constitutes the prototype of the earliest human environment:

> This environment. . . is probably undifferentiated; on the one hand, there are as yet no objects in it; on the other hand, it has hardly any structure, in particular no sharp boundaries towards the individual; environment and individual penetrate into each other, they exist together in a 'harmonious mix-up'. (1979, p. 66)

There is the foetus and there is a physical medium (the amniotic fluid), but we cannot say whether the medium is outside or inside the foetus nor can we ask which came first; self and environment are completely 'mixed up'; they interpenetrate each other. Whilst birth ruptures this undifferentiated state and inaugurates the process whereby 'objects, including the ego, begin to emerge from the mix-up of substances and from the breaking up of the harmony of the limitless expanses' (p. 67) this process cannot occur immediately, for the task of the earliest phases of infant life is to discover a new medium, a primary social medium, within which the journey of human life (as opposed to the foetus's purely physical life) can begin.

According to both Balint and Winnicott, the role of human nurturance is to re-establish in social form the sense of undifferentiatedness which was the reality of the foetal environment. This requires the establishment and maintenance of an illusion for the infant is now in reality separate. To have a good start in life we need to be 'let down' gently; otherwise the realization of our being 'set apart from' (our destiny as the world's only truly trans-formation beings) would be unbearable.

This illusion is the first creative act in which we participate; it is our first contribution to the human culture in which henceforth we shall be increasingly immersed. Winnicott's detailed description is unsurpassable:

> at some theoretical point early in the development of every human
> individual an infant in a certain setting (normally) provided by the
> mother is capable of conceiving of the idea of something which would
> meet the growing need which arises out of instinctual tension. The infant
> cannot be said to know at first what is to be created. At this point in time
> the mother presents herself. In the ordinary way she gives her breast and
> her potential feeding urge. The mother's adaptation to the infant's needs,
> when good enough, gives the infant the illusion that there is an external
> reality that corresponds to the infant's own capacity to create. In other
> words, there is an overlap between what the mother supplies and what
> the child might conceive of. . . Psychologically, the infant takes from a
> breast that is part of the infant, and the mother gives milk to an infant
> that is part of herself. In psychology, the idea of interchange is based on
> an illusion. (1951, p. 239)

From this perspective therefore the primary narcissism and omnipotence
of the infant is a joint construction, endogenously and exogenously determined, neither properly internal nor external but both. Winnicott (1952)
refers to this as a third space, lying between and drawing upon both the
space of our internal world and of external reality, the site of culture and
of intersubjectivity. It is the moment at which the infant first dips its toe into
'the pool of humanity' (a phrase Winnicott repeatedly uses).

The earliest experiences of nurturance, if they go well, recreate the
merged phenomena of intra-uterine life. In place of the physical medium
in which it was once suspended, the infant now finds itself held in the
embrace of the other who cares for it and whose adaptiveness provides the
infant with the illusion that reality is, as it were, under magical control. We
cannot yet speak of this other as an object; rather, it constitutes what we
might describe as a benign background or Balint's 'friendly expanse'. By
virtue of this primary social medium, the infant is, according to Winnicott,
able to do what an adult would call relaxing:

> The infant is able to become unintegrated, to flounder, to be in a state
> in which there is no orientation, to be able to exist for a time without
> being either a reactor to an external impingement or an active person
> with a direction of interest or movement. (1958, p. 34)

This quiet sense of being is, then, derived from the earliest experience of being merged with the post-natal environment. An experience which is, as we have seen, an intersubjective phenomenon; a joint creation of infant and nurturing figure. Intersubjectivity therefore precedes subjectivity. Without this original 'secure sense of being' the infant cannot properly 'emerge', that is, become 'set apart from'. The task of development is to be 'set adrift' from this position, to become psychically what one is already physically – a separate human being yet securely in contact with one's social being. Winnicott captures this through his phrase 'to be alone but in the presence of others': the task of development is at first the internalization of this sense of a benign presence so that one might be alone yet able to represent (make present again through some form of representation – a cot, a chair, an atmosphere) this otherness which is a part of one's own being. In this way we can move from being abjectly dependent upon others' support towards being 'self-supporting'.

Experiences from adult life, however, suggest that this quiet sense of being is a most precarious one. We know from the experience of psychotherapy and from the dramas of the unstructured group that for many adults, possibly a good majority, the discovery of our basic intersubjectivity is extraordinarily difficult. We seem to need constant reassurance. The absence of trust, considered in this most essential of its forms, seems striking. As a consultant in group settings it seems I am constantly having to say 'the medium will support you if only you will let it'. It would seem that perhaps the majority of us were never 'let down gently' but rather had the repeated experience of being dropped into a sea of experience which threatened to engulf us. It is at this point that we can usefully leave Winnicott and turn to Bion for whilst, as we noted at the beginning of this argument, his concern is very similar to Winnicott's, he approaches it using a different language with a different sense of life.

Not being a philosopher, I could not say what tradition Bion draws upon as he attempts to develop a theory of mind from his early clinical work with groups; from his work with schizophrenics in the 1950s and, finally, from his work as a training analyst in his later years. Bion himself mentions Kant; others describe or accuse Bion as being a neo-Platonist. I have few scruples in this area which might get in the way of listening to what I feel he is trying to tell us. The gist of his message seems to me to be a very simple one, although its simplicity is masked by the irritatingly difficult form in which it is conveyed. Although at times one thinks the worst of him, I do not think

Bion deliberately sets out to make things obscure. His use of language is probably marked by his awareness that its purpose is as much for dissimulation as communication: better for the reader to make 'no sense' rather than the 'wrong sense'.

Given that the thrust of Bion's work is an enquiry into what enables us to think about experience, perhaps the best way I can convey my under-standing of his work is to explore my own experience of reading him and the processes involved in reaching some understanding. For me the over-whelming experience has been one of prolonged periods of frustration punctuated by periods of quiet but temporary satisfaction. Now you might say that this experience is common to anyone endeavouring to come to grips with a complex piece of writing. In part, I am sure this is true, but I have always found that there is just enough in Bion's work to keep me tantalized, to reinforce a belief or a faith that he is endeavouring to communicate at the very frontiers of what, through language, is communic-able. At first very often it was no more than a throwaway phrase, passage or way of describing things. To give an example: speaking of the impact of hatred and envy Bion insists that it destroys the possibility of conscious contact either with self or other as 'live objects'. He continues:

> Accordingly we hear of inanimate objects, and even of places, when we would normally expect to hear of people. These, though described verbally, are felt by the patient to be present materially and not merely to be represented by their names. This state contrasts with animism in that live objects are endowed with the qualities of death. (1962, p. 9)

Not only is this a poetic description of a part of the phenomenology of psychotic states, moreover it threatens to extend vastly our understanding of representation and communication and introduces the idea of a mental process (in which meaning is stripped away from digested experience – a kind of petrification process) which I feel is quite novel to Western thought. I still do not fully understand what he is saying here, but each time I read this I feel good. I know there is something to be grasped, but I cannot quite get hold of it. In Bion's terms, I have a preconception, a conception which is 'not yet'; thought exists, but I cannot yet conceive of it. The absent conception tantalizes. As a nothingness it is a very real something; its 'somethingness' is felt 'somethingness': 'it' gnaws and frustrates like a hunger. I can be patient or I can give up. Indeed, I have given up on many writers who have frustrated me but never also made me feel good. Giving up on people who give you only bad experiences is easy, but to give up on the good without being tempted to disparage or dismiss them is very hard. I am reminded of what often happens in groups who have grown accustomed to toiling away in the darkness when someone shouts, 'Eureka!' The strange thing is that more often than not this does not mobilize group fellow feeling and love; rather, the group comes to hate that person with all their guts. 'Why should he "have it" and not me? It's not fair, we should all be ignorant together, blessed are the self-blinded! Let us be noisily triumphant in our affliction and deride those who claim to see or who persist in the delusion that sight is possible.' I am reminded here of Bion's (1962, p. 95) description of the function of -K, namely 'to demonstrate that an ability to misunderstand is superior to an ability to understand'.

However, I have gone on a bit. Let us return to my difficulties in conceiving of what Bion means; a difficulty which gnaws at me like hunger. According to Bion we are always subject to two hungers. From the outset, as natural beings, we hunger after the physical nourishment necessary to sustain us as a form of animal life, but as human beings we also hunger after an understanding of our own experience. All infants require these two forms of nourishment. I am now more or less in a position to describe what for me is the gist of Bion's thinking. There are, it seems, three interlinked arguments:

1 Experience always tends to outstrip our capacity to contain it.

2 Whilst we might thirst after truth, 'to understand' is, more often than not, 'to suffer'. Thus, whilst they might poison the mind, lies preserve us from conscious suffering.

3 At the very beginning we have no internal capacity to transform our experience into something which is both bearable and nourishing; we are completely dependent on those who nurture us for this. If it is true that we are transformative beings then this is the very first transformation, a transformation in which the raw material of experience is made digestible for us. This seems like the origin of all human labour. I like to think of it as 'the labour of love'.

Bion's *first proposition* implies that in relation to the fragility of the human psyche life is always potentially traumatic. One is reminded here of Freud's constant return to the theme of trauma. We often think of his early clinical writings here (1896) or of his return to such themes two decades later in

Beyond the Pleasure Principle (1920). Perhaps, less obviously, much of his structural theory, particularly his conceptualization of the ego, assumes an environment which tends towards the traumatic; hence his notions of the 'contact barrier' and of the 'protective membrane' or 'shield' and so on (1923). But whereas Freud could conceive of such phenomena only in intrapsychic terms, Bion is able to examine them as interpsychic phenomena, that is, as regulatory functions performed by those who nurture the infant who at first has no equipment for processing experience at all.

Comparing Winnicott and Bion one is struck by the former's optimism. Not that Bion sees life as hopeless, but he draws our attention to the darker side much more than Winnicott. To my mind, Bion is the first analyst to have given a convincing description of the working of the death instinct in everyday life in a way which is concrete rather than abstract. But he also draws our attention to the sheer intensity of human experience and not just to the more obviously traumatic incidents that pertain to parental or other forms of violence. What is meant, then, by the notion that from the outset experience always tends to outstrip our capacity to contain it? Let me try to illustrate my understanding of this through an example. It relates to an incident which is obviously traumatic but, I hope it will be agreed on reading it, the real violence here is that which is done to humanity. The following incident was reported briefly in a national newspaper some twelve years ago:

Tower block deaths fall

A mother and her two young children died yesterday after falling from the ninth-floor balcony of their flat in a West London tower block.

Mrs Elizabeth Anderson, aged 30, and her daughter Tracy, aged 4, were found dead at the foot of the block – Frank Powell Court, Bedfont Lane, Feltham. Her other daughter Samantha, aged 5, died on the way to hospital.

Neighbours said they were awoken at 1.30 am by screaming. Mrs Lesley Burt, 23, said she heard one of the girls scream: 'I don't want to go, Mummy.'

Mrs Burt said she heard noises from Mrs Anderson's flat but thought it was just an argument.

She later heard the police arrive. Mrs Burt said: 'I looked out of the window and saw a woman and two little girls lying on the ground.'

Mrs Anderson and her children landed on grass outside the ground-floor flat of Mrs Joyce Hill. 'I heard a child shouting "No, no, no" then I heard a thump hitting the balcony rails,' said Mrs. Hill. 'Just as I was about to call my husband I heard another two thumps.'

'I looked out of the window and saw what I thought was a pile of clothes, not realizing it was three bodies.' The two little girls were dressed in their nightclothes.

Over the years I have read this repeatedly and still I cannot come to terms with it. Somehow or another I feel I owe it to this little family to try to understand what happened to them. I suppose I want to make it better, but I know I can't do this for the dead, only for that part of them that still lives on inside of me. I find the little girl's words, 'I don't want to go, Mummy,' so hard to bear. How could we have let that happen, to that woman, to those children? Maybe years ago things were easier. The problem with mass communications is that they confront us with experiences we have few means of thinking about. Incidents such as these seem inconceivable, no method of understanding seems capable of containing them. And so we choose either to deaden ourselves by attacking our own capacity to be sensitive beings or to struggle to comprehend and use the scraps of understanding so gleaned as a means of healing the rents and wounds opened by events which are beyond our grasp. Freud always said that without the pain there can be no pleasure. *Thinking through things can be a profoundly painful business* – really to think of the loss of someone who was close, of hurting or of being hurt, of personal defeat or humiliation, is to realize that love, attachment and commitment are always potentially unbearable; really to love someone is to know already of their loss. But these things have always existed. Some things are, however, quite new. The 'radical evil' of the death camps and gulags is new, and so is the possibility of exterminism.

I first came across Primo Levi's writings not long before he too was found dead on the ground below his balcony. As an Auschwitz survivor he had much to tell. His problem was that to tell of his experience he had to find ways to thinking of it and thence reliving it without being overwhelmed. In *The Periodic Table* (1986) he hooks individual episodes out from the dark pool of his memory using the elements of the periodic table as metaphors in which each event could safely be put to rest. In *If This Is a Man* (1987) he tries to take us close to what happened, not to rub our noses in it but to help us think of it. One senses, however, 'a distance' in his description and some things are never mentioned. The essay opens with a verse which is, I feel, his only explicit confrontation with us, the only moment where his passion takes us to task:

If This Is a Man

You who live safe
In your warm houses,
You who find, returning in the evening,
Hot food and friendly faces:
    Consider if this is a man
    Who works in the mud
    Who does not know peace
    Who fights for a scrap of bread
    Who dies because of a yes or a no.
    Consider if this is a women,
    Without hair and without name
    With no more strength to remember,
    Her eyes empty and her womb cold
    Like a frog in winter.
Meditate that this came about:
I commend these words to you.
Carve them in your hearts
At home, in the street,
Going to bed, rising;
Repeat them to your children,
    Or may your house fall apart,
    May illness impede you,
    May your children turn their faces from you.

Note how he calls to us from beyond the warm houses of our own experience. Whether our civilization still retains the capacity and willingness to imagine pain, to stay with it, think through it, this to me seems crucial. We are all of us now in a life-or-death situation. Bion knew this, and I feel that is why he places the struggle between life and death at the centre of his psychology. We can choose life with its pleasure and pain or we can deaden ourselves and betray the future. His work, for me, is therefore not just a psychology; it is a morality. He invites us to live and suffer, rather than to choose comfort and psychical death. From this choice none of us is excused, no matter how hard the circumstances.[2] Levi knew this too. Towards the end of *If This Is a Man* he recounts an incident where all the work squads of Auschwitz are assembled in the parade square to witness a hanging. The man to be hanged took part in a rebellion at Birkenau; he was being made an example of. The squads watched the hanging in silence and marched back to their huts. They were the survivors, but there was not a strong man left among them. Oppressed by shame, they could not look each other in the face.

Bion traces the struggle between life and death as moral orientations right from the beginning of infancy. The infant is hungry and becomes distressed. In the beginning it has no means to contain its own experience. It has no 'inside', no internal space and time in which experience can be held and digested. In this state, experience cannot provide the infant with food for thought. Without assistance things go in one end and out the other, or out the same way they came in. The psyche lacks dimensionality. As Meltzer *et al.* note (1975), we speak of failure of attention or concern in adults in terms of 'things going in one ear and out the other'. And what comes out is more or less the same as what went in; undigested experience, like undigested food, is fit only for evacuation.

In the beginning, then, the infant evacuates experiences through its distress that it cannot digest or assimilate. It hungers after food and after an understanding of its own experience. The parent receives this double hunger and feeds the infant both physically and with her love. We would say that she 'makes it better'. She takes hold of the infant's distress, holds it in her arms, suffuses it with her love. In this way she works upon the raw material of the infant's experience, breaking it down, enveloping it with her understanding, transforming it into something palatable enough to be returned to the one she cares for.

This act of love is the very first labour, and by virtue of it the infant travels from the physical universe of sensation to the psychical – and therefore social – universe of symbolized experience. Again one is reminded of Freud's notion of the anaclitic relationship between the self-preservative instincts and eros, the life instinct. Eros leans upon this original preoccupation with physical self-preservation to lead the infant into the mysteries of humanness. This fusion of material and psychical satisfactions is crucial yet can so easily be subject to a splitting process whereby material comforts come to simulate psychical satisfactions. Excessive dependence on material comforts thus suggests an atrophied hunger for understanding.

This first labour of love Bion describes in terms of the dialectic between container and contained: the contained being the undigested experience the infant evacuates through its distress; the container being the enclosed space that receives it, modifies it and makes it tolerable. In the beginning this space is the embrace of the mother or nurturing figure, it is neither a physical space nor a social and emotional space but both, that is, a naturally social space. If the infant is to be helped along the path to understanding its experience – from bad physical sensation to the realization 'hunger', from 'bad breast present' to the idea of a 'good breast which is missing' – then this embrace should not be so anxious and rigid that the infant's experience cannot be fully contained nor should it be so loose and inattentive that the experience slips or seeps through its grasp.

From Bion's point of view the first task of development is the introjection of this container into which one's experience was previously reliably placed. As Bick (1968, p. 484) notes, until 'the containing functions have been introjected, the concept of a space within the self cannot arise'. This, then, is the achievement of self-containment; of having the sense of a self contained within a boundary which is more or less permeable. Bick is probably doing no more than extending Bion's logic when suggesting that this containing object is experienced concretely as skin.[3] Indeed, we are reminded here of Freud's insistence that the ego is 'first and foremost a bodily ego; it is not merely a surface entity, but is itself the projection of a surface' (1923, p. 16).

The vista that Bion is opening up before us is breathtaking. For the first containing embrace of the mother's body is the prototype not only of our own internal capacity to contain experience and reach some understanding of it but of an endless series of internal and external substitutions from the body of the family and the group, to the body of the motherland and to the body of Christ. Moreover, through this original labour of love emerges the first conception, the first re-presentation. This is the idea of the breast missing, which provides the first internal 'something' that the infant is capable of holding on to in order to contain its own hunger. Each subsequent representation is marked by this essential form of being a skin or body which contains meaning. As Bion suggests:

Learning depends on the capacity of the container to remain integrated and yet lose rigidity. This is the foundation of the state of mind of the individual who can retain his knowledge and experience and yet be prepared to reconstrue his past experiences in a manner that enables him to be receptive to a new idea. (1962, p. 93)

Bion's conception of the container–contained relationship therefore provides the basis for a dialectic of knowledge. It is because experience always tends to outstrip our capacity to contain it that each symbiosis between experience and thought threatens to become a mutual entrapment and each insight a form of imprisonment. To quote Bion, 'the recurrent configuration is of an explosive force within a restraining framework' (p. 79). As Meltzer (1978, p. 104) adds, for development to occur a 'language' must be found 'not necessarily verbal, that can both contain the idea without being exploded by its pressure of meaning nor be so rigid as to compress the idea and thus reduce its meaningfulness'.

The final term from Bion's language we should consider is his notion of patience. When earlier I spoke of my personal experience of reading Bion I mentioned the patience he demands if one is to make any sense of him. For Bion, the prototype of patience is the infant's capacity to tolerate frustration when hungry. The infant's struggle to contain its own hunger is synonymous with the adult's struggle to contain the frustration of 'not knowing'. We speak of the gnawing presence of doubt, of ideas not 'coming together'. For Bion, the infant with its double hunger and the parent that provides both physical nourishment and primitive food for thought constitute the original 'thinking couple'; the first 'coming together' of a preconception (that is, a 'not yet' conception) and an experience which is capable of giving birth to meaning (the idea of the breast missing). Again our language is revealing if we only stop to think of the two distinct meanings of 'to conceive of' or 'conception'. Here then is eros as concrete manifestation rather than as abstraction which, 'by bringing about a more far-reaching combination of the particles into which living substance is dispersed, aims at complicating life and at the same time, of course, at preserving it' (Freud, 1923, p. 30).

Patience, then, requires the toleration of doubt and the ability to bear a fragmentary understanding. Drawing on Klein's schema of the paranoid-schizoid and depressive positions,[4] Bion likens the process of human development and the evolution of cultural thought to a recurring oscillation between phases of integration and disintegration. For Klein the paranoid-schizoid position characterizes the earliest phase of development in which the infant has no conception of the one who nurtures it as a whole, coherent figure. Rather, it experiences fragments of understanding (part objects) organized around the dynamic of splitting, projection and idealization. The realization that the one who cares and nourishes is the same one that frustrates and deprives, that this figure is not ideal but real and hence fallible, announces the arrival of the depressive position. It is at this point that relationships with whole objects (persons) properly begin and the infant's experience moves from incoherence to coherence. The experience of not knowing, of having only bits of understanding, thus finds its proto-type in the paranoid-schizoid position and its attendant persecutory anxieties (we speak of being persecuted by doubt). If patience cannot be mobilized sufficiently then we succumb to anxiety and reach for premature solutions. Such solutions cannot be syntheses, rather they are forced congelations of relatively undigested particles. Only with patience can we give birth to (conceive of) a new organizing idea; it cannot be forced, it has to be allowed to emerge. Bion uses a phrase from Keats to contain the meaning he seeks to give to patience: 'when a man is capable of being in uncertainties, mysteries, doubts, without any irritable reaching after fact and reason' (letter to George and Thomas Keats, 21 December 1817).

For Bion, then, patience is equivalent to toleration of anxiety; an anxiety that gnaws at the bones, tightens the shoulders and makes the heart feel raw. It is the kind of anxiety elicited in groups and organizations at the point of disintegration, as chaos and rumour stalk the corridors, and people start to use words as spears. To stay with the anxiety in situations like this and keep alive the capacity to think, the capacity 'not to lose your mind', is what Bion means by patience. We are clearly talking here of the experience of crisis – in Bion's terms, where the restraining framework threatens to collapse around the explosive force it had previously contained. And Bion is not simply thinking here of the context of personal life, but equally of the life of a group or political party or, indeed, of society itself. As Meltzer (1978, p. 107) notes, Bion pictures the inner world in a way which makes clear 'that the concreteness of psychic reality has the same texture as the concreteness of politics, that life and death of the mind are as much in the balance in the one as life and death of the culture "and its beneficiaries" are in the other'.

We are a tension: a tension between a desire to know and a desire not to be disturbed; between the nourishment of truth with the pain that this incurs and the desire for comfort, for that warm house of quiet experience. And it is from this vantage point that Bion totally reframes all existing psychoanalytic metaphors. There are now just two actors on the stage, the scientist and the liar (Bion, 1970, Chapter 11). And, whilst the former courts collapse through seeking development, the latter tirelessly erects fortresses of consolation upon the fissiparous sand of experience. Seen from here all human defences are lies, the necessary little stories we tell about ourselves. The task, for each one of us, is to be just enough of a liar to make life bearable whilst sustaining a certain openness to experience. Each lie, being a deadening of experience, is like a deadening of life itself. Although he never makes it explicit, Bion's experience of the first seventy years of the twentieth century, perhaps particularly his personal acquaintance with the full horror of combat in the First World War,[5] leaves him bleakly pessimistic about our willingness to choose life in an era of destruction.

There is a fine balance to be struck here. The patients in Bion's consulting rooms had renounced life in order to survive; they had become lost in a vast labyrinth of lies that had been frenziedly constructed to stave off psychical collapse. And in this lay their predicament, for each new extension to the already obsolete containing framework in the long run merely contributed to the explosive pressure of development.[6] To choose life we must deaden ourselves but only sufficiently to remain comforted in our discomfort; to make disintegration, when it comes, a manageable disintegration. We know, from our study of individual lives and from our experience of civilization, that this is no easy thing to do. Lest we all become 'dead men on leave' we must quickly learn to choose survival a little less and life a little more.

NOTES

1 As with other areas of psychoanalysis a number of insular traditions of analytically informed group work exist in a country like the UK. The tradition I am concerned with here could legitimately claim to be the most classically orthodox. Its roots lie in Bion's work during and after the Second World War and in the so-called 'Leicester Conferences' which began in 1957 and continue to this day (now jointly sponsored by the

Tavistock Institute of Human Relations and the Tavistock Clinic) and in the USA through the work of the A. K. Rice Institute. If you want to get some idea of how you might behave 'after the bomb had dropped', attending the two-week Leicester event should surely give you some clues.

2 But there is another side to this and a lighter one. For if it is difficult to conceive of pain it is no less difficult to conceive of pleasure. To enter the human universe is to partake in a mystery in which much of life will remain beyond our grasp. Lyotard (1984) refers to such experience as 'the sublime' and urges upon us the search for new presentations in order to 'impart a stronger sense of the unrepresentable'. This is the area of play, Winnicott's 'manipulation of reality in the service of the dream'.

3 The notion of 'the skin' as the origin and prototype of the experience of surface and boundary has emerged strongly within the Kleinian tradition over the past twenty years (Bick, 1968). Judicious use of this concept could provide important insight into the structure, function and psycho-pathology of space in the physical environment of home, community and urban landscape. A recent article by Szekacs (1985) may prove illuminating here.

4 These two positions constitute the essence of Klein's reformulation of Freud's developmental theory. There have been innumerable sum-maries and elaborations but probably one of the most original and accessible can be found in Ogden (1986, Chapters 2, 3 and 4).

5 See Bion's (1987) remarkable autobiography of his early years, *The Long Weekend*.

6 One cannot but be struck by the parallel between Bion's dynamic schema here and Marx's own concept of contradiction, particularly as construed within the dialectic of the forces and relations of production.

5

Everyday 'States of Mind'

NORMAL MADNESS

The application of psychoanalytic insights to the study of phenomena outside the consulting room – culture, consumption, politics – has always run the risk of reductionism. This is particularly so where the attempt has been characterized by the search for a few 'universal explanations' of complex social phenomena. One thinks, for example, of Schneider's (1975) account of the culture of mass-production capitalism in terms of the simple category of 'anality'. When too much meaning is forced into a conception in this way it inevitably spills out. The category simply cannot contain all that is being asked of it; it becomes saturated, soggy and loses its capacity to hold the limited sense it might otherwise effectively procure. But even where psychoanalytic insights are applied sparingly, where their domain of applicability is clearly specified and their heuristic value secured by a clear-headed and realistic appreciation of the boundaries beyond which such insights destroy rather than create meaning, even here we face problems regarding the generalizability of the phenomena of the consulting room. Put crudely, the central problem seems to be this: how can we move with ease and confidence from the dynamic internal world of 'the patient' to the world of what might be termed 'collective pathology'? How can we generalize from our analysis of the world of the autistic child or the successful but 'borderline' adult personality to what often seems like the madness of normal life, whether we consider this in terms of our complacency in face of the prospect of mass extinction, the development of intimate attachments to inanimate commodity objects or the collusion of otherwise intelligent and sensitive workers in the maintenance of depersonalized human institutions?

The very term 'collective pathology' indicates the problem we have to struggle with here. Were the nurses in Menzies' (1959) classic analysis of the endemic depersonalization process at work in her hospital case-study mad? Clearly they were not 'mad' in the sense of requiring treatment. They appeared to live normal lives outside work. Did they become 'mad' only when passing through the hospital doors to begin their shifts? Menzies uses the term 'social defence system' to refer to the existence of institutional processes which emerge to protect staff from a reality which is hard to bear. Despite the pioneering nature of this study, it nevertheless suffers from a naivety or blindness to contextual issues. The task of nursing is, by its very nature, an emotionally exacting one. As Menzies notes, the ordinary nurse daily confronts the most difficult kinds of social interaction imaginable, with both patients and their families. They are involved in the most intimate fashion with people in pain, undergoing processes of decay, confronted with loss or facing death, and, on the other hand, experiencing the joy of birth or the relief of recovery. What Menzies fails to make clear is that the task of nursing is made more or less difficult according to the social context in which it operates. The task of nursing is more difficult if performed within a society which itself has not been able to come to terms with illness, death, sex and intimacy. The task of nursing is made more difficult if the profession itself is run on regimented lines, subordinate to the feudal baronies of medical consultants, according to a culturally established professional ethic which fetishizes the maintenance of professional 'objectivity', 'distance' and so on (Ehrenreich, 1978). Add this to a British National Health Service which since its inception has been resourced just sufficiently to provide adequate levels of servicing whilst precluding the possibility of actual human service (Hoggett, 1988; Waddell, 1989) and one gets some sense of a social context, still largely unchanged twenty-five years on from Menzies' study, which makes a difficult task a virtually unbearable one.

By ignoring the social context in which work is performed, psychoanalytically informed analyses of institutional processes inevitably veer off in a reductionist direction: one particularly thinks of Jaques' (1951) studies of factory systems in this light. What we require are forms of analysis which seek to examine the interrelation of psychic structure and social structure, the 'subjective' and 'objective', the internal world with the external world. Specifically, in the study of everyday life, I wish to demonstrate how the psychoanalytic notion of 'states of mind', a notion first given substance through Melanie Klein's concept of developmental 'positions', provides the basis for understanding what I would describe as 'madness in normality' – precisely the kind of phenomenon that Menzies was trying to elucidate in her analysis of hospital institutions.

Psychoanalytic practice, the work of the consulting room, has been primarily concerned with the examination of states of mind as they express themselves in terms of fixed and unchanging personality complexes. Thus it tends to speak in terms of 'the borderline personality', 'the psychotic personality' and so on. To take psychoanalysis beyond the consulting room into the world of culture, politics, group and organizational life, we need to entertain the possibility that states of mind, besides having a certain biographical fixedness, may also operate at a collective level. We might think therefore of the existence of 'collective states of mind' invoked within particular social contexts.

I would argue that it only became possible to take psychoanalysis out of the consulting room when Kleinian and object-relations theory developed classical psychoanalysis in a direction away from Freud's early energy model of the psyche. My feeling is that the attempt by Marcuse and others to use this early model as the basis for a critical social theory was fundamentally misconceived, for Freud's early model construed the mind as an essentially closed system of endogenously generated impulse, fantasy and structure. In Freud's later work, and one thinks specifically of 'Mourning and Melancholia' (1917b) and *The Ego and the Id* (1923), a second and essentially intersubjective model of the psyche emerges. It is a model which not only allows for the penetration of the external into the internal but, more radically, insists that the development of the person is only conceivable as the effect of the interpenetration of endogenous and exogenous forces. Whilst Klein perhaps never satisfactorily resolved this contradiction within Freud's own work, she nevertheless provided the basis for the future development – through the work of figures such as Winnicott, Bion and Meltzer – of a properly relational model of psychical life. In place of Freud's psychological monadism the discipline of psychoanalysis begins to refocus upon a new object: individuals in relationship.

The emergence of the object-relations and post-Kleinian tendencies therefore announces a shift in the psychoanalytic gaze from the mythological closed system of the energy and oedipal model to the dialectical play between internal and external worlds. While each pole of this dialectic is discrete, having its own rules of structure formation which are irreducible to the rules which govern the opposing term (Hoggett and Lousada, 1985), neither pole of the dialectic can stand on its own; each term – internal and external – while discrete, acquires its proper meaning only through the other; meaning occurs by virtue of 'the couple'. In this light we can consider a 'state of mind' as a fundamentally relational phenomenon, that is, as a mode of relationship between internal and external realities. Fairbairn, Winnicott and Balint were absolutely consistent on this point; it was expressed through their rejection of the very possibility of a state of primary narcissism[1] (of a state of primary unrelatedness to the world). Similarly, if we consider Meltzer *et al.*'s (1975) notion of dimensionality in human functioning, even the most primitive level of 'autistic two-dimensionality' can be described in terms of its relational form (adhesive identification). If we follow the logic of this shift in emphasis rigorously then it becomes clear that 'states of mind' are constructed by the relational couple. Winnicott (1951) understood this clearly when he noted how the earliest phase of infant development, a phase of apparent undifferentiatedness, was in part the outcome of the nurturing figure's work of illusionment. We might wonder, then, whether the partners in this process of construction are always and necessarily equal. What if, far from complementing the developmental requirements of the maturing psyche, the external partner demands compliance with its own 'state of mind'?[2] If we begin to move away from the ideas that states of mind are necessarily endogenously created then these are the prospects we can begin to contemplate.

Let us return now to the issue with which we originally sought to come to terms. How can we understand apparently mad behaviour undertaken by apparently normal individuals? Forgive me for using the extreme example which follows, but it crystallizes the issue because of its very nastiness. How can we understand the man who sits at home with his family in the evening, plays tenderly with his youngest children, but during the day works as an administrative or technical officer in an extermination camp? Primo Levi (1986) encountered just such a man, Müller, the officer in charge of the Buna chemical lab at IG-Farben works. It was built alongside Auschwitz, from which it drew its slave labour; that was how Levi met Dr Müller. Decades later Levi wrote the tragic tale of his accidental encounter with Müller. They corresponded but never met. Müller wrote that during his sojourn at Auschwitz he 'had never gained knowledge of any proviso that seemed aimed at the killing of Jews' (p. 221). Levi remarks that

Müller's statement seemed 'paradoxical, offensive, but not to be excluded'. He adds:

> At that time, among the German silent majority, the common technique was *to try to know as little as possible, and therefore not to ask questions.* He too, obviously, had not demanded explanations from anyone, not even from himself, although on clear days the flames of the crematorium were visible from the Buna factory. (1986, p. 221)

Reflecting on his correspondence, Levi makes a judgement about the man Müller: 'Neither infamous nor a hero: after filtering off the rhetoric and the lies in good or bad faith there remained a typically grey human specimen, one of the not so few one-eyed men in the Kingdom of the Blind' (pp. 221–2).

Levi's *The Periodic Table* was first translated into English in 1985. The same year, John Steiner, a British psychoanalyst, published a paper entitled 'Turning a blind eye' (1985). Although Steiner's paper had clearly been written before the appearance of Levi's book in Britain, the commonality of their concern is striking. The title of Steiner's paper is drawn from his reflections on recent reinterpretations of Sophocles' *Oedipus Tyrannus*. The classical view beholds Oedipus as a victim of fate vainly pursuing the truth. Steiner, however, calls our attention to the possibility that everyone knew who Oedipus was from the start: the story of Oedipus is thus the story of a cover-up, one with which Oedipus colludes until circumstances make it difficult to maintain the evasion any longer. Steiner then draws parallels between such a reinterpretation of the myth and experiences in his consulting room. He talks about patients who have insight and gain knowledge of their internal predicaments yet nevertheless deny the significance of their own truthful experience. Steiner links this process of denial to the work of an internal propaganda machine which puts forward ingenious arguments why the patient's own better knowledge need not be taken seriously. Steiner (1985, p. 168) notes: 'Chance seems to play an important role in this process, as it forms the vital flaw through which the truth can be attacked. Everything may point to the initial truthful observation but it has not been proved beyond doubt; there is still a chance that it may be wrong.'

Was this also the case with Dr Müller? Is this also the case with the silent majority, the grey men and women who prefer to turn a blind eye? Steiner does not hesitate to draw such conclusions regarding a range of social issues including, above all, the imminence of ecological or nuclear catastrophe. We know of all these things, yet the significance of our own better knowledge is denied. Like Steiner's patient, our insight seems to make no difference to our propensity to repeat actions which lead to familiar painful outcomes. Steiner characterizes this mode of being in relationship to the world as dishonest and perverse. Amazingly, Levi, however, has it in him to offer an element of forgiveness, even to those like Müller who stand by. With touching humour he notes, 'it is not easy to be one-eyed'. Levi thanks Müller for his honest endeavour 'to settle his accounts'. In reply to Müller's request that Levi make some judgement of the German's behaviour. Levi replies:

> I admitted that we are not all born heroes, and that a world in which everyone would be like him, that is, honest and unarmed, would be tolerable, but this is an unreal world. In the real world the armed exist, they build Auschwitz and the honest and unarmed clear the road for them... after Auschwitz it is no longer possible to be unarmed. (1980, p. 223)

How, then, can we conceptualize the state of mind of 'the unarmed', of those who prepare the road? We are speaking of a mode of evading truths that are difficult to bear. In the post-Auschwitz, post-Hiroshima world we all inhabit, it is a truth which is always there, always in the background, never entirely out of sight. It is like a curse; our only consolation being just the chance that it will not matter. This is not psychosis for, as Steiner noted, the truth is not completely evaded, but neither is it neurosis where reality is for the most part accepted.

We can neither accept reality nor can we deny it; we can neither accept that this really is the world we live in nor can we deny it. Of course we know the facts: about overkill, proliferation, the 'ozone hole', and so on; but they lie there before us strewn across the ground looking ridiculous. 'Surely you cannot mean me to take you seriously!' They look preposterous, like huge shrivelled-up fruit, drained of vitality and significance, hanging about, waiting. But don't pick one up; it will explode in your face. Stay cool, don't look too serious, don't get too involved. There was just a chance that those flames were not really from Jewish bodies. Did six million really die? Would they really use those atomic weapons? Will they really let the tropical forests be destroyed? It is through little holes like this that the meaningfulness of an almost unbearable world drains away.

I have used this extended example in an attempt to give meaning to the concept of 'state of mind' and to argue that it constitutes a mode of relationship between internal and external worlds which not only finds expression in the transference dynamic of the consulting room, but also at the level of mass psychology. I hope my method does not seem reductionist. As I see it, the usefulness of psychoanalytical case studies is that they reveal in detail, as it were under a microscope, information about broader social sentiments and orientations which otherwise remain diffuse and boundaryless. As to the question, 'Is the mass sentiment simply the aggregation of individual dispositions, or are the individual "states of mind" merely a reflection of broader cultural phenomena?', I believe our only response is to refuse to answer, refuse to be drawn into the rules of this game of split human discourse.

As I have argued earlier, we should not necessarily think of 'states of mind' as fixed and unvarying modes of being we carry around with us from situation to situation. For most individuals there is an intimate relationship between 'state of mind' and social context. So far we have looked at just one social context, that is, where our own better knowledge proves difficult to bear. We have observed how it tends to elicit from people an orientation to the world which is neither psychotic denial nor neurotic acceptance but one which is on the borderline of the two. But before we investigate this relationship between state of mind and social context any further, we must pause and consider this psychoanalytical concept in more detail.

'STATES OF MIND' IN PSYCHOANALYSIS

I have found Ogden's recent work illuminating here (1986). He reminds us of the absolutely essential step taken by Klein and Bion when breaking away from the notion of developmental stages implicit within classical psychoanalytic theory. Speaking of Klein's concept of the paranoid-schizoid and depressive positions Ogden notes: 'These "positions" are not passed through but, rather, continue throughout life as co-existing modes of organizing and processing experience…each generating a distinctive quality of being' (p. 52). In other words although these positions are en-countered sequentially (one cannot enter the depressive position before first being in the paranoid-schizoid position), once encountered they are never 'left behind'.

Each position – autistic, paranoid-schizoid, borderline and depressive – therefore constitutes an organized mode of relationship between internal and external reality only one of which, the depressive, is properly subject-ive; the others express varying degrees of pre-subjectivity. We might think therefore of each state as being equivalent to a basic human predisposition or mode of apprehension of external reality, and from this perspective we can see how psychoanalysis can provide an essential element for any critical social theory. The task becomes one of studying how particular social contexts alter the internal relation of forces between these predis-positions, bringing some into the foreground, pushing others into the background. In other words it becomes possible to see how some situations make a properly subjective position difficult (if not almost impossible) to sustain. This is not just an issue of violence and repression for, very often, situations induce, seduce or reduce us into a pre-subjective position. Moreover, the constant interplay between external and internal reality suggests that the 'balance of forces' which contribute to the entrance of one state of mind and the departure of another must always be understood as constituting internal as well as external forces. We are never free from having to face our own responsibility.

In an extended footnote Ogden (1986, p. 42) attempts to sketch the constituent elements of a 'state of mind'. Each state of mind or position constitutes a particular mode of experiencing both external and internal reality (the quality of which, he suggests, is a reflection of the degree of subjectivity that has been achieved). The quality of this experience will relate to the psychological *location* of the individual's subjectivity in rela-tion to his or her body, thoughts, the not-I, the psychological *space* available for thinking, dreaming and fantasizing and one's sense of *place* in relation to one's past and future. Finally, there is the degree of differentiation of one's self, one's symbols and the symbolized. Because each mode of experience is never left behind but coexists with other modes encountered later on during the course of development we can begin to see how, from this perspective, the personality appears to develop laterally rather than vertically. In opposition to the idea of the personality as something which is built upwards from a primitive base, where each developmental stage constitutes an overlay or stratum upon the previous one, we are invited to consider it as a series of adjacent modes of organization, all still in the process of construction, even though work began on some before it began on others. From this point of view regression is not a 'going-back' to a previous state but, rather, is a displacement, or moving across from, one dominant state of mind to another.

We have, however, still to grasp the full meaning of the idea of Klein's positions as 'coexisting' modes of organizing and processing experience. So far we have still construed 'coexistence' in either/or terms; that is, either one state of mind is operant or another one is. But this assumes sequential coexistence rather than simultaneous coexistence. In the latter case we would be able to entertain the idea of the coexistence of a number of different modes of relationship with the world all occurring at the same time. From this perspective we need to think of the relationship between different states in terms of dominance and subordination rather than presence and absence. The achievement of the depressive position therefore is not equivalent to the (temporary) absence or surpassing of the paranoid-schizoid state; rather, it is equivalent to the ascendancy of a new mode of organization which reorders and repositions all earlier constructions; that is, it puts them in their place.

At times Bion approached the conceptualization of group phenomena in precisely the same way. The group moves through a series of basic assumptions (or positions) any one of which may become dominant at a particular moment in time. But even when a given basic assumption is dominant, it still has about it 'a quality that suggests it may in some way be the dual or reciprocal of the other two' (Brown, 1985, pp. 209–10; Bion, 1961, pp. 165–6).

BIOGRAPHY: INDIVIDUAL AND COLLECTIVE

This analysis of subjectivity developing in a lateral direction, outwards rather than upwards, has so far been posed in terms of an ideal-type of normal development. In other words we are assuming that the Dr Müllers of this world are reasonably normal people who are forced to occupy particular states of mind in order to cope with particular life events which they may either face uniquely or, as is more often the case, face in common with many others. What we have not examined is the predisposition of individuals towards particular states of being. We have assumed so far a range of states of mind (autistic, paranoid-schizoid, borderline, depressive) in conjuncturally determined relations of domination and subordination *vis-à-vis* one another. What we have failed to consider so far is the individual's own biographical circumstance, that is, the particularities of his or her own personal history. This clearly is the essential terrain of routine psychoanalysis. It tells us that one's biographical circumstance influences the particular valency or pulling power that given 'states of mind' have within the personality. From this perspective we may speak of a personality being essentially borderline or autistic; that is, relations of dominance and subordination between different states of mind always have, to some degree, a biographical fixedness. More recently, particularly as a consequence of the work of Bion (1957b), psychoanalysis has also been able to see the way in which relations of dominance and subordination may correspond to internal spatial structures. Sydney Klein (1980), for example, points to the existence of 'autistic cysts' within otherwise borderline or neurotic patients. If we think of the internal world as we might think of an external social territory, we can speak, then, of autistic enclaves lurking within a predominantly depressive regime, as localized internal spaces within which alternative regimes are dominant.

My particular focus here, however, is with everyday life; with what, at a given point in time, passes for 'normal living'. I am seeking to interrogate just what we mean by 'normal living', given that, when psychoanalysts such as Menzies have turned their attention to normal social forms such as the hospital, things turn out to be not quite so unproblematic as the term 'normality' would suggest. Through the metaphor of 'turning a blind eye', we have already explored a particular state of mind, defined clinically as 'borderline', which provides some insight into the functioning of those who just 'stand by'. Elsewhere (Hoggett, 1986) I have endeavoured to examine the nature of our dependency on society's technological and social infrastructure. As I argued then, the silent hands which bring food to the supermarket shelves and electricity to the home are only ever noticed when they fail to provide for us. It is only at such moments that the ruthlessness of our dependency becomes clear through the hatred felt for a background object which has dared to assert its autonomy.

Civilization seems skin deep, but are we right in seeing the problem in terms of a thin and punctured veneer of civilization through which we constantly slip into the barbarism below? Perhaps 'civilization' does not deserve such credit. Many have noted the disparity between humankind's technical powers and its psychological immaturity. There is now a tradition of psychoanalytically informed social critiques of modern civilization which seek to analyse this disparity through the medium of the idea of collective psychopathology. It is a tradition which originated with the work of the Frankfurt School and its studies of *The Authoritarian Personality* (Adorno *et al.*, 1950) and finds contemporary expression in the work of writers such as Christopher Lasch in his analysis of *The Culture of Narcissism* (1978). The common theme of these critiques is their attempt to construct a theory of collective psychopathology through the analysis of an assumed bio-graphical predicament produced by dislocated socialization processes in Western culture. Lasch, for example, traces the origin of this predicament to the way in which paternal authority has been undermined by the commodification and 'statification' (i.e., the process of hegemonization by the state) of the family. The development of mass communications and mass consumption presents the developing child with a host of real and fantastic identificatory figures against which the father seems like a very mundane ideal. On the other hand, the massed ranks of media experts and pundits, and the professionalization of education, child care, leisure and health, undermine the legitimacy of paternal authority.

The role of the father as limit and ideal, as the locus of the law and the vehicle of possibility, becomes weakened and thereby, also, does the super-ego. In its place emerges an archaic ego-ideal (reminiscent of Chasseguet-Smirgel's maternal ideal) and super-ego (functioning according to the principle of 'talion morality' rather than 'depressive morality'), pivots of a personality within which neither desire nor destructiveness recognize any boundedness.

From Lasch's point of view a scar had fallen upon the collective bio-graphy of our children. Like the Frankfurt School, he positions the family as the essential medium through which economic and social developments impact upon the human personality. I feel this line of reasoning has much to commend itself. What concerns me about it, however, is that it is still inclined towards reductionism in its methodology. The contemporary world just seems too complicated to be encapsulated within a single category, even when, as with Lasch's analysis of the culture of narcissism, that category is articulated with great depth and richness. I wish to come at things from a different direction, one which seeks to examine irrationality in everyday life and culture without accounting for it in terms of an assumed rupture of collective biographical circumstance. Specifically, I wish to argue that certain objects, regimes and settings are themselves so bizarre, trau-matic or extraordinary that they have the power *to draw us into* certain states of mind. From this point of view a critique of contemporary civilization should be built upon *analysis of* the way in which it attacks and destroys our subjectivity in the present, in the here and now, irrespective of any possible mediation through our biography.

The idea that certain regimes, objects or contexts exert a force upon the individual personality, affecting the relationship of dominance and subordination between the various states of mind, is, I believe, compatible with Bion's attempts to rethink the way in which psychoanalysis constitutes the human subject. His early seminal paper 'Differentiation of the psychotic from the non-psychotic personalities' (1957b) reformulates subjectivity as a construction necessarily containing both psychotic and non-psychotic elements. The establishment of the latter is always a matter of 'more or less' rather than 'either/or'. The psychotic organization is never entirely left behind in 'normal' development or rather, putting it more strongly, the non-psychotic element is never entirely secured. Indeed, Bion's pessimism leads him to wonder whether, given our experience of twentieth-century civilization, we have the subjective capacity to survive as a species. It is because the dominance of the non-psychotic element is so fragile, so subject to contestation, that humankind may not always set itself only those tasks which it has the capacity to solve. On this issue, for entirely personal reasons, I feel Marx's optimism is to be recommended. The danger with Bion's despairing vision is that it tends to disarm us. The alternative, surely, is to agree with Levi that the future is in doubt and to arm ourselves accordingly.

The usefulness of Bion's view for the argument I am elaborating here is that, if the dominance of the non-psychotic organization is always subject to contestation, it may only require a nudge to upset it. Indeed I wish to go further than this, for I feel the notion I have just put forward is still too crude to illuminate the possibility that in the course of a single day any given individual may inhabit a variety of states of mind – some through choice, some involuntary – many of which are the consequence of direct attacks upon his or her subjectivity. To proceed any further with the argument, some time must first be spent considering in more detail than has been done so far the character of these 'states of mind' as modes of relationship between the internal and external world.

THE PHENOMENOLOGY OF 'IT-NESS'

Klein's unique contribution to the development of psychoanalysis lies in her adumbration of the two fundamental positions through which subject-ivity is constructed. I do not wish to describe these positions in any detail – the paranoid-schizoid and depressive – for this has been done elsewhere, and many times. What I do want to do is investigate the phenomenology of these positions.

The paranoid-schizoid position represents a pre-subjective world in which internal and external 'objects' exist to which attitudes are adopted (such as flight, attack, incorporation) in an unmediated way; that is, in a way unmediated by an interpreting, meaning-giving subject. To understand this state of being from the inside, as it were, is extraordinarily difficult. This, I feel, is the value of Ogden's (1986) account of Klein's positions; his description is consistently imaginative and enables us to get a glimpse of each state by translating Klein's often mechanistic language into an ordinary one.

Contrasting the paranoid-schizoid and depressive conditions, Ogden argues that whereas in the former 'everything is what it is... in the de-pressive position, nothing is simply what it appears to be' (p. 73). Ogden links this to the issue of perspective. To gain any kind of perspective on things which provides the object with depth and reveals dimensions which are otherwise not visible, it is essential to be able to assume more than one position (considered here as standpoint) *vis-à-vis* the object. This implies the existence of some space, in this case a psychological space, in which a subject can move around. Ogden refers to this as the space 'in-between' the self and its experience, that is, the space for thought. Thought is representational. In other words, its fundamental character is to re-present, make present again in mental space, the material of experience. If experi-ence cannot be represented it can only 'be present' in an immediate and unmediated way, and in this sense it is experienced as bombardment. As Ogden (p. 27) notes, 'The infant's thoughts, feelings and perceptions are conceived of. . . as constituting things-in-themselves, events that simply occur', and later, speaking of the paranoid-schizoid position, he argues that it 'is a developmental phase of "it-ness" wherein the infant is lived by his experience. Thoughts and feelings happen to the infant rather than being thought or felt by the infant' (p. 42). This, I feel, accounts for the particular form of persecutory anxiety (according to Klein, the anxiety appropriate to this position) as fear of intrusion or invasion. Because the ego is still archaic and relatively unformed, because the infant is still reliant on the 'auxiliary ego' function of a nurturing figure which, even at this early stage, is already embarking on its path of disillusionment, the self is too thin-skinned to cope with much of its experience without being damaged. In Klein's terms, the infant feels persecuted by its bad objects. In the context of analysis we sometimes see the same phenomena posed in terms of the analyst's experienced intrusiveness.

From this perspective it is incorrect to equate the paranoid-schizoid position with denial of reality, for in one sense, at this point in development, reality (whether the reality of internal or external experience) falls like hail upon the unprotected shell of the infant psyche. What is missing is contact with human reality, that is, meaningful reality. This is the achievement of the depressive position. If we think of ourselves as naturally human (as having a 'human' nature) then within the paranoid-schizoid position it is nature which still dominates; we are, if you like, not yet properly humanized. The human element of human nature is inscribed through the emergence of our subjectivity, but whilst this construction is in its early stages we inhabit the state of being of the 'self as object.'

The depressive position is thus equivalent to the establishment of the 'self as subject'. A self which, rather than merely being the focus of sensation within a world which 'just is', has the possibility of observing and creating its own thoughts. Freud's distinction (1915b, 1917b) between thing-presentations and word-presentations is helpful here. In the paranoid-schizoid position the word-presentation rather than being a re-presentation of the thing becomes a thing in itself. Thoughts become things, ideational globes or accretions of ideational stimuli. Rather than 'standing for' something, they are something. There is no differentiation here between the thoughts and the one who thinks. We might say the individual is too closely identified with his thought and feeling experiences. Rather than forming material which can be worked upon, the individual 'is' his experience. To say that an individual is lived by his experience is equivalent to saying that he is 'thunked' by his thoughts, occupied by them, invaded or engulfed by them; he is not thinking thoughts or having thoughts; rather, he is had by them. It strikes me that this may be part of what Bion (1962) means when he argues that thoughts precede the construction of an apparatus to think them. Thoughts precede the thinker who is, at first, 'thunked' by them, feelings precede the feeler who is 'feeled' by them.

So, from this point of view, the paranoid-schizoid position is characterized not so much by its thoughtlessness as by its *mindlessness*. The world is not senseless; if anything, it is 'senseful'. However, the sense it is full of is 'bad sense', that is, sensation without meaning. If, within this position, the infant is out of his mind, it is not because he has lost it; rather, he has not yet found it. Only later, through regression, may we speak of people 'losing their minds', for this statement then assumes the existence of something which once existed but was then lost.

An example may help us understand the status of thoughts in the paranoid-schizoid position. Consider an institution where the majority of staff are occupied by the thought that 'no one is more abused by this organization than me', but where no thinkers exist to think through this thought. For the individual, the evidence is incontrovertible. We can deduce this from the fact that each individual seems fixed by two complementary attitudes. The first of these is consciously held: each feels persecuted by 'the institution', even though, because of its smallness and informality, one is hard put to discover 'an institution' over and beyond the individuals who have created it.

The second attitude is less consciously held but can be inferred from the behaviour of the group. The recurring complaint of staff members refers to the feeling of being isolated, of not being able to 'come together' with other colleagues. This experience of fragmentation is publicly blamed on the institution; privately, if probed, some individuals will admit to the intensity of rivalrous feelings towards colleagues; others react with outrage at such a prospect. Subsequently, an organizational consultation reveals the full extent of the envious contempt and hatred these 'colleagues' hold for each other. The consultant acts as 'the apparatus for thinking' that which otherwise cannot be thought. Through her intervention individuals are released from their position of compliance before 'incontrovertible facts'. Until this point feelings were facts to be acted upon, not elements of an experience which needed to be understood. Feelings, such as 'others are only looking out for themselves' or 'no one really knows what it's like to be in my position', were not material for exploration but facts impelling modes of action-secretiveness, reserved distance, negativism. Thoughts existed but in a form whereby the thinker could get no distance from them, they could not be put into perspective or viewed from another angle. These are 'concrete thoughts', hard and unmalleable. They cannot be used for thinking. They do not represent anything; rather, individuals make themselves present in and through them. Here, actions, do not speak louder than words; instead, they fill the space where words might otherwise be. In a sense, to an outsider who retains the capacity for thinking, the actions of such individuals are truthful, but they express a truth which cannot be grasped by those who act. In groups such as this it is better to speak a true word than repeat actions whose truthfulness is inconceivable. Is experience to be represented in a way which invites exploration or is it to be presented as fact, as 'the truth of the matter'? This is the difference between good sense and bad sense, between the depressive and the paranoid-schizoid positions.

THE TYRANNY OF ROUTINIZATION

In *Learning from Experience* (1962) Bion poses an essential question: are the events we experience in our internal and external worlds to be responded to as facts requiring action or as problems or mysteries that invite our understanding? By insisting on the centrality of Klein's epistemophilic instinct in human and social development, he broke away from Freud's simple opposition between the Pleasure and Reality Principles, a framework within which curiosity, the desire to understand, assumed a necessarily secondary position as a facet of the Reality Principle (Meltzer, 1978, p. 42).

Bion therefore begins to develop a picture of the pre-subjective world, a world in which the apparatus for thinking either does not yet exist or has been destroyed. By elaborating upon the Kleinian notion of the concrete-symbol (Rodrigue, 1956; Klein 1930), he enables us to break out of our presumption that the existence of symbols is equivalent to the existence of understanding. Alongside the idea of the 'meaningful representation' he places the idea of the 'meaningless representation', the 'meaningful misrepresentation' and the 'representation as thing-in-itself' (that is, as the 'real'). From such a base Bion then begins to launch a systematic assault upon the way in which we 'take for granted' the routines of everyday life, a life which is as much about the destruction of the capacity 'to make sense' and the preservation of an attitude of mindlessness as it is about the provision of a stable form of containment for going-on-being. As he notes, language appears to be designed as much for the purpose of dissimulation as for the expression of truth!

We need then to rethink the dynamics of everyday life and such institutions as family and work that constitute its fabric. We need to understand such everyday institutional routines as fundamentally Janus-headed: as both support and as trap; as life-sustaining and deadening. To view everyday routines and conventions simply as a defence against ontological insecurity, as Giddens (1979, p. 219) and other social theorists do, is to miss the point. Whilst they certainly perform such a function they do so at a price – and the price to be paid is subjectivity itself. Moreover, mental pain and anxiety are not overcome by the use of such social defence systems. As Menzies (1959) noted in her study of hospital institutions, such social forms of emotional containment are in themselves compromise formations, allowing only for the reproduction of 'symptomatic behaviour', behaviour through which the conflict between impulse and control, chaos and order, is managed without being resolved.

An adequate critical theory of routinization must therefore always bear in mind its darker side, for it is only from this perspective that we can examine our complicity in a way of being which constantly threatens to capture us as inert, mindless and non-reflexive selves. From this perspective, routinization, particularly when considered in its recursive form, is the essential expression of 'it-ness' in everyday life. Our inability to sustain an attitude of thoughtfulness when faced by the complications of life contrasts with our facility for technical thinking, where reality is inanimate and devoid of such complication. This threatens to be the cause of our downfall. We live in a world whose technical capacities increasingly threaten to overwhelm our ability to understand the question of their social value and consequences.

Giddens uses the concept of 'recursivity' to characterize the routine nature of everyday life, yet he relates recursivity to notions of habit, convention and repetitiveness in a way which draws our attention away from the other side of recursivity, that is, its circularity. This other side refers to the prevalence of 'vicious circles' (Masuch, 1985), 'games without end' (Watzlawick *et al.*, 1968), 'parasitic relationships' (Bion, 1970) and so on, as a prevalent feature of everyday life in family and organizational systems. In particular, it draws our attention to something which at first seems quite paradoxical: the frenzied and compulsive character of many aspects of

everyday routine. We are reminded particularly of Freud's notion of repe-
tition-compulsion which finds expression both in his theory of psychic
trauma (1920) and in his observation that children cannot have their
pleasurable experiences repeated often enough. Thus we need to develop
a picture of everyday routine as something both inertial and restless. It
demonstrates both the tendency towards tropism and the desire to return
to the state of the inorganic, but at the same time it is ceaselessly active. I
would go so far as to say that there is a frenzy and incipient irritability to
much of this mode of being which is quite exhausting; indeed, its outcome
often appears to be inertial exhaustion. An example may clarify my
argument.

Not so long ago I was on a train returning from Manchester to Bristol. A
family got on at Cheltenham: a mother, a teenage friend and three children.
The children demanded drinks, the mother refused; they demanded more
loudly, a 'compromise' was reached – they could have their drinks if they
'behaved themselves'. The drinks were bought and one was promptly spilt,
hostilities escalated and subsided; a game of impossible requests ('just sit
still'), transgressions, verbal lacerations and sulking ensued. This conti-
nued, without interruption, for the full forty-five-minute journey. I alighted
at Bristol with a searing headache. Is this what Lyotard (1984) means when
he speaks of communication as 'agonistics'? Clearly the illustration exemplifies Bion's notion that language is often used as a mode of action,
'intended to disencumber the personality of accretions of stimuli and not
to affect changes in the environment' (1962, p. 13). What was going on in
this family? It felt like they were gobbing and kicking at one another, using
verbal and non-verbal means of communication as modes of combat;
although they obviously found it distressing in a strange sort of way it was
also pleasurable to them.

Despite its violence this family interaction pattern was very stable. It
functioned as a closed system of actions and reactions in which forces both
impacted upon one another and had a repercussive effect within the family
group as a whole. I have a picture of the 'domino rally' in mind, where one
domino is tipped over onto another which in turn hits another and so on.
If the line of dominoes is arranged in a large circle then the last domino in
the circle falls upon the domino which began the whole movement, and
the pattern repeats itself. We may think of such forms of circular motion as
they find expression in the timeless drama which unfolds when father
returns home from work after a bad day. Father collapses in a chair and

reaches for the newspaper. The youngest child attempts to climb on his lap but meets with rejection. We might say that at this point the child has an experience which her own mental apparatus is unequipped to think about (a normally loving father has reacted coldly and dumps his 'bad day' into her). Unable to create a space internally from which this experience can be considered as material for mental work, the experience is projected out-wards into another (the child runs to mother and starts demanding her attention). The other may experience a bad little girl, hold these feelings and make it better or may react to this experience by scolding the bad little girl who, for no apparent reason, has started to become extremely irritating. If the other reacts in this way she ends up feeling bad herself for scolding her irritating child. She in turn may start to irritate X, and so on.

In such closed interaction loops behaviours reverberate throughout the system until someone resorts to understanding rather than action. The alternative is either a game without end, an 'explosion' or the tendency to drive one of the players crazy. Clearly the latter possibility has provided the basis for many of the contemporary developments within family therapy. Chiesa (1986) notes the concern within the various schools of family therapy to examine 'circular holistic patterns' in what are often not only closed but absurd interaction systems. He notes that not only is the game endless and paradoxical but the main rule is that nobody can win. He adds the useful insight, 'It is impossible to gain unilateral power in a relationship which is by definition circular' (p. 33).

A critical theory of routinization must of necessity draw attention to the restless circularity of everyday life. But we must also look beyond the form of movement within repercussive interactions to the question of just what it is that is being carried by this motion. Speaking of what he calls the 'reversed family' Meltzer *et al.* (1986) observe that in interactional systems where action is resorted to rather than understanding, 'mental pain (almost entirely persecutory) tends to circulate in the intra-familial pecking order eventually to be evacuated into the community by predatory actions' (p. 167). Hinshelwood (1989) uses the term 'affective communication net-works', to describe this process by which affect-laden bits of experience, lacking a thinker to perform the mental work necessary to transform them into meaningful communication, are passed around in a kind of perverse language game. Although easily confused, we need to distinguish, there-fore, between the circular motion of many everyday routines and the circulation of affect which is achieved through such movements. Interes-

tingly enough, Hinshelwood (1989) develops this notion of affective communication networks as a means of understanding everyday behaviour
within institutional settings. Whilst most of the theory of interactional
circularity has been developed primarily by those seeking to understand
family dynamics there is every reason to believe that the same phenomenon
underpins the inertial basis of much of institutional life. Indeed, there is
good reason to believe that Bion's basic assumption groups operate in an
analogous fashion. If this speculation is in any way valid then it must lead
us to conclude that the circulation of affect within social systems is not
limited to persecutory anxiety but may also be relevant to catastrophic and
depressive anxieties.

A final characteristic of recursive social systems worth examining is
indicated in Chiesa's (1986) remark that they seem to operate according to
a game rule which dictates that nobody can win. In terms of the classical
Prisoner's Dilemma model, recursive social systems operate primarily on
the lose/lose principle rather than the principle of 'you win some/you lose
some', let alone the principle of 'mutual gain'. The following is an example
based on my experience of consultancy with a political organization trying
to hold itself together in the face of defeat and demoralization.

This particular group was in control of the government of a city district
which was reeling from attacks on it by the Conservative Central Government in the UK. The group was rapidly dissolving into rival factions,
resulting in a paralysis of its capacity to take any effective action on its
internal or external environment. In this context it seemed that political
energy was being invested primarily in efforts to make sure other factions
did not win. Any kind of 'trading' between factions appeared to be impossible; indeed, this factionalism was rapidly seeping into the factions
themselves. In this situation 'the enemy within' was becoming far more
vivid and alive than 'the enemy without'. Because everyone had a target in
their sights, everyone was also a target in someone else's sights; because
everyone was distrustful everyone was paranoid, every hunter was a victim,
and so on.

Summarizing our experience of working with this group, we wrote at
the time:

Regarding conduct and relationships with the group, the basic issue was
lack of trust and an ambivalent attitude towards leadership of any sort.
People's socialist values didn't seem to inform in any way how they

behaved towards each other. No single individual (eg Chair) could have a hope of re-establishing more fraternal rules of conduct, this has to be a collective responsibility. Put bluntly, the track down which you were heading seemed to us to be one best described as 'mutually assured destruction' – exactly the course Thatcher has planned for Inner City Labour Parties around the country. This may offer the consolation of being seen to be 'going down fighting', but you leave the real enemy entirely unscathed!

The example is particularly interesting because of the way in which it illustrates the link between destructive circularity and the process of 'turning in upon oneself'. There is a peculiar imploded quality to many of the families, groups and organizations we have been examining here, and whilst this may be the result of conjunctural impacts (that is, particular events which precipitate withdrawal from engagement with external reality), there is good reason to believe that this may also be a consequence of the structural positioning of such institutions. The privatized nuclear family, for example, seems ill-equipped to carry the weight of emotional experience it is forced to bear. For the vast majority, work offers little in the way of emotional satisfaction; it is a means to life, not 'life' itself. Even for those, such as professionals, for whom work provides some form of enrichment the sheer arduousness of the job is such that they return home drained and frustrated – as anyone who knows a nurse or teacher will testify. If we increasingly look to a world outside work for the realization of life, then it must also be admitted that the modern family constitutes an increasingly restricted and fragile space within which such satisfactions can be nourished. As Poster (1978) notes, historical research on the family, its form and structure, suggests that the status of the family as the heart of the private sphere is a comparatively recent phenomenon. It presumes the existence of a 'world of work' outside, and set apart from, the family; it presumes the former 'private–public' sphere of everyday life built around the integration of family, kinship and community has been ruptured. In its place now stands the discrete space of 'the private', increasingly occupied by the atomized family, and the discrete space of 'the public', a space increasingly synonymous with simulated communities of consumption, mass communications and the state. The more that the real fabric of everyday social relationships is destroyed, the more such simulated forms of relationship insinuate themselves.

Besieged by unmet emotional needs and constantly subject to invasion by the alien public forces of commodification and 'statification', the atomized family, as the site of individual struggle for self-emancipation, resembles an increasingly unlivable situation (Collier, 1977, p. 136). This, then, is what I mean when I suggest that the structural position of many everyday social forms may account for a good deal of their imploded quality.

HISTORICITY AND SUBJECTIVITY

The basic anxiety of the depressive position lies in the realization of the value of good sense – one's own and others' – and the inevitability of one's attacks upon it. We are all imperfect creatures struggling to make sense of a reality which is difficult to bear; the reality of one's own family as well as the reality of the modern world. No one is free from the solace that bad sense and nonsense bring; these little lies that we tell ourselves seem so preferable to the pain of thought.

We might consider thoughts and feelings as the basic material of human experience. The depressive position is then equivalent to a state of mind in which the individual subject can make use of her own material of experience – work on it, chew it over, process it. In other words, it is only at this point in development that a subject exists capable of engaging in mental work independently of the labour of what we might call her 'nurturing auxiliaries'. As Ogden notes, in the context of the analytical relationship we speak of the shift from repetition to remembering, from being the object of our own personal history to being its reflexive subject. He adds, 'The process of transforming enactment into remembering… is at the heart of what Freud (1932) meant by… "Where it was, there I shall be"' (1986, p. 82). Lukàcs (1971) speaks of class consciousness in terms of the shift in position achieved when a class moves from being the object of history to its consciously co-determining subject. In an analogous fashion, we can think of the achievement of the depressive position as that in which the individual shifts from being the object of her own personal history (that is, her biography) to its co-determining subject. But because the paranoid-schizoid position is never 'left behind', the individual never abandons the position in which she is, in part, the object of her own personal circum-stance. Subjectivity is, therefore, always a matter of degree; the self-as-subject and self-as-object always coexist. The struggle of subjectivity can therefore never be complete. Nor is this simply a question of value, that is, that subjectivity is somehow or other to be preferred to 'it-ness'. Rather, the former cannot exist without the latter. That step into freedom – the sense of taking responsibility for one's own actions, of making choices to which one is unavoidably accountable – would be impossible without the sedimented and crystalline form of our own biography, a personal history of interlocking constraint and self-constraint. As Ogden (1986, p. 83) suggests, it-ness is not simply resorted to out of fear, as a defence from the fear of freedom; rather, it is an essential part of our being, the nature within our human nature. To repeat, we are humanly natural beings, subject to nature and subjects of nature. Klein's two positions are equivalent to the psychological registration of this ontology.

The shift from re-enactment to memory in the context of analysis implies historicization. As Meltzer (1978, p. 79) notes, most analyses begin with the recitation of facts about one's personal history, but so long as those facts remain facts the analysand remains bound within his own prehistory. The mental work of analysis is concerned with the discovery of meaning and significance; it is only through this process that prehistory becomes 'his story'. Whether we speak of the emergence of the self-as-subject or the class-as-subject we are speaking of the recovery of memory and history, the transformation of a bundle of unconnected facts and silences into an authentic hypothesis – firm enough to provide the basis for further exploration without being so rigid that the possibility of other vertices is precluded: 'The history we are left with can never be considered as an absolute term, as the "truth" substituted for the lie. The endlessness of the historicization process is what finally makes the analysis "interminable"' (Baranger *et al.*, 1988, p. 125).

ROUTINIZATION AS A FORM OF HEGEMONY

So far so good, but we have not yet reckoned with the effect of power and terror. For the process of historicization threatens the rule of 'the establishment', the grey men of the Pentagon and the Brezhnev era, no less than 'the establishment' within. Meltzer *et al.*'s (1986) illuminating examination of Bion's notion that the psychical world derives both its form and dynamic from its status as a kind of internal society provides a means forward for us here. The brilliance of some of the argument is such that I feel no diffidence in citing the following extract at length:

> Here is an imaginative conjecture based on Bion's extraordinary one: suppose that the primitive BA level of the mind, organized as an 'establishment', if strong enough, may have direct access to those complex humoral, haematological and healing processes which ordinarily protect our bodies from the various noxious events which threaten them. Suppose further that this 'establishment' treats these processes to which it holds, or claims to hold, direct access and the monopoly, as a 'privilege' which it dispenses with an open hand to the 'obedient' self. Suppose further that in order to survive in the internal and external worlds it is necessary for the thinking parts of the personality to acquiesce in the rules of the two 'establishments', internal and external, and to make for itself, quietly as it were, elbow-room in which to carry out the passionate interests and relationships that are the heart of the life-in-the-mind. If at some point an enlargement of this elbow-room were to take place which ran counter to the requirements of the internal 'establishment', might the individual find himself in a kind of legal-political trouble exactly analogous to that pursuant to a 'breach-of-the-peace' or 'anti-State activity' in the outside world? Might the thinking parts of the personality find that the privilege of immunological products had been cancelled and that everyday processes of defence against bodily enemies, external ones like bacteria, for instance, or internal enemies like primitive cell mutations, no longer operated. It would be similar to one's water or electricity being cut off. The house would soon become uninhabitable unless archaic modes of coping could be revived. (Meltzer *et al.*, 1986, p. 39)

We must begin to think, then, of the possibility that hegemonic processes operate both internally and externally. And, moreover, that the internal and external establishments may be involved in an active process of collusion. From their point of view mindless subjects are much to be preferred to those who have recovered both memory and desire.

I have argued that our objectness, our 'it-ness', should be considered as an essential aspect of our being, the mark of our 'naturalness'; a nature which we can never properly emerge from, given our corporeal and physical character. But we must now reckon with the power of the establishment and its effect in creating a surplus-objectivity (apologies to Herbert

Marcuse!). One of the paradoxes of civilization therefore is that it appears to progress by keeping humanity primitive: mindless beings, buffeted by incomprehensible forces, trapped within recursive biographical loops. I say 'appears to progress' advisedly, for we might wonder whether this concept of progress is not also a conceit of the establishment. It was Trotsky (1921), no less, who noted that civilization has no divine right to progress. If the hegemony of the internal and external establishment is too complete then a collapse into barbarism is the consequence. It was in this way that Ancient Rome collapsed; it took us a full thousand years to recover. In this way, too, feudal Polish society collapsed and only now may it be recovering its vitality. Who can doubt that today the whole of our civilization stands on the brink of barbarism. In times like these we no longer have the right to be mindless. The issue, however, is not simply one of survival, as Lasch and others have noted; the real issue is the survival of life-with-value. The pressures of everyday survival seem intense enough for most of us, yet the key question is not how to survive but for what purpose? Once the question of purpose, of value, is put foremost we may well risk our own death, certainly the destruction of our life-chances (career, etc) as the cost of doing what is necessary. However, I leave aside the question of whether we should be willing to risk others' lives or life-chances, largely because I cannot find any answer to this that leaves me feeling easy.

For development to proceed, for truth to triumph over the lying propaganda of the establishment with all its threats, its promises and its blandishments, a force must exist capable of pushing forwards with its own work of transformation. A thoughtful establishment, one with the grace and humility to understand that it does not have the last word, cultivates the forces immanent within it which will bring about its own destruction. As Gramsci once said, the best leaders have one foot in the grave. For dwelling within every lie, a truth lurks; every act of concealment and dissimulation affirms the existence of the very experience it seeks to hide. This dialectic of negation and affirmation is revealed by Bion through his notion of the inevitability of the true thought and the unimportance of the individual who harbours it. We speak of 'ideas whose time has come'; Bion (1970, p. 105), adds, 'even if it requires a thinker it does not require a particular thinker and in this resembles truths – thoughts that require no thinker'.

In this light we can see now that the task of analysis is to make imminent what before was only immanent. The traditional image we have is one of 'bringing things to the surface'. This is a twofold task: on the one hand there is the job of clearance, of removing the concealments, interrogating the propaganda, deciphering the secret codes; on the other there, is the job of making contact with 'the underground', giving it encouragement and providing it with knowledge of enemy movements. We are drawn always to considering the balance of forces, whether in the life of the mind or in the life of society. So there is no teleology here; the movement from immanence to imminence is not inevitable but a matter of struggle between contending forces. Moreover, the explosiveness of truth may bring about collapse just as easily as transformation. As we can see in the Soviet Union after the 'August coup' of 1991, the process of disintegration must be contained if development is to be the outcome.

As Meltzer *et al.* note, the establishment works hard through its propaganda to construe the forces of change in terms of 'the mob'. It promises order and control, 'a sense of security and pleasure is achieved and the price being paid is hardly noticed' (1986, p. 48). Speaking of 'Miss E' they note that the dichotomy between order and chaos, between the mob and the establishment 'seemed not to have any middle ground to form a spectrum of social organisational possibilities' (p. 45). Whether we consider the internal or external world the problem, then, is whether an agency exists to harness this explosive spontaneity, synthesize it, provide it with the words it lacks to fuse its love and aggression into an objective rather than objectless force. Regarding the psychical world, Meltzer and colleagues appear to picture this agency in terms of the existence of good internal parental objects capable of allying themselves with 'the idea' in its struggle with the establishment (p. 48). We might think also whether this combined parent figure (strong but gentle) is not the model for the group or agency in the external world most capable of leading social movements in an effective struggle against the external establishment.

CONFUSIONAL STATES

The concept of 'the confusional state' has been extended and developed primarily through Klein's (1930) early work on symbol formation. For Klein, the infant first discovers its external world through a process of symbolic equation. As Rodrigue (1956) put it, the child is driven by its oral impulses to see 'a mother' in every object. The infant's interest in the world is then essentially an externalization of its interest in the mother; exploration of the world's boundaries and textures is equivalent to an exploration of the 'insides' and 'outsides' of this original object. If development proceeds well enough, then the infant will reach the point where symbolic equation can give way to symbolic representation. At this point symbols cease to be presentations of the original object but become the means by which an absent mother can be represented. As Rodrigue (1956) notes, representation assumes the existence of an absence which can be called back into mind.

This early process of symbolic equation constitutes the prototype for later states of mind encountered in adult life: specifically the confusional states associated with psychotic breakdown. Segal (1986, p. 49) gives the example of a schizophrenic who, when asked by his doctor why he had stopped playing the violin, replied, 'Why? Do you expect me to masturbate in public?' As she noted, psychotic breakdown altered the situation in which the violin had functioned as a symbol used for purposes of sublimation to one in which it had become a real presentation of an original object, his penis. Segal and others refer to the way in which, in confusional states, words and objects lose their symbolic value and become 'concrete objects'. In this situation the signifier becomes 'the thing signified'. The boundary between reality and fantasy has become confused and broken down.

Moving now from the individual to the social we can see how this concept of 'confusional states' can be applied to an examination of the modern world. I would like to spend some time in discussion of contemporary developments such as post-modernism. Before doing so it would be useful briefly to consider two other achievements of the late twentieth century which, in a diffuse but, I believe, very real way, conspire to undermine our collective ability to discriminate between fantasy and reality.

When Kovel (1983) speaks of 'the state of nuclear terror' he has a double sense in mind: as a powerful technocratic state formation and as an internal state of terror. One of the earliest attempts to register the effect of this state of nuclear terror upon everyday life was Jeff Nuttall's *Bomb Culture* (1968). Nuttall's book was one of the first of that long line of works devoted to an analysis of 'pop culture', but in this case the focus was primarily upon the 1950s (the period of his late youth). Speaking of the studied affectlessness, casual violence and explosion of style at that time he notes:

But it would be false to dismiss the culture and the role as being merely a mask. It was a mask whose quality was particularly appropriate, being neither the image of our inward terror nor the image of the outward lie, but being, rather, the image of the sour, dynamic discomfort it was to contain such hypersensitive solitude. (Nuttall, 1968, p. 23)

In 1911, before the two World Wars, before Hiroshima, Freud examined the 'end of the world' fantasy of Schreber; a fantasy in which Schreber believed himself to be the only one surviving, the human shapes and figures around him being 'miracled up, cursory contraptions' (Freud, 1911). To begin with, Schreber was convinced that the earth's allotted span was only another 212 years; towards the end of his stay in Dr Flechsig's sanatorium 'he believed that the period had already elapsed'. I do not wish to dispute the validity of Freud's judgement that Schreber's state of mind was clearly delusional, although Schatzman (1976) has provided a convincing reinterpretation of the 'Schreber' case which demonstrates the way in which the hapless Schreber may only have been carrying the madness of others, especially his father. However, if Freud were alive today and faced with the same 'patient' one wonders whether he would be quite so confident in judging Schreber's belief system as delusional. Surely some would say today that 212 years is itself so naively optimistic as to be deluded. There is a saying, and I believe it originates from somewhere near Disneyland, that capitalism has the capacity to make your wildest dreams come true. Truly, this cannot any longer be doubted. Freud could conceive of Schreber's state of mind only as being the product of an internal catastrophe. The question we must ask, when we overcome our desire to dismiss it as exaggeration, is whether the fantastic reality of the late twentieth century has created within each one of us, irrespective of biographical circumstance, a place perhaps sealed or encysted, of catastrophe, brimful of terror and despair. Is it any longer possible to know who is more deluded than whom?

The second development I would like to note, which again juxtaposes intimations of terror with the destruction of any means we might have of 'reality testing', concerns the development of the apparatus of the secret state. I realize that Britain under Thatcher perhaps qualifies as a special case here, but even in the USA, where formal constitutional rights and civil liberties remain largely intact, the secret state and its techniques of surveillance bring about another dislocation of our reality sense. For whilst it is surely paranoid to believe that one is being watched and monitored, it is no less irrational to deny the existence of an external agency which in reality may be watching, listening, manipulating and deceiving. As Janine Puget (1988) notes, in the context of the Argentinian dictatorship, the destruction of the capacity for 'signal anxiety' was one of the essential means by which the state disarmed its population.

Now I reckon myself to be a fairly rational person. I do not have sleepless nights thinking about good friends who may turn out to be double agents or of the possibility that someone from MI5 is fiddling with my bank account (though I do wonder where all the money goes). I have never thought of joining the Liberty (formerly National Council for Civil Liberties) nor do I scan bookshops for the latest analyses of the secret state apparatus. I always considered those interested in such issues to be a bit paranoid; I think they possibly were. But given that, by the very nature of its secrecy, we have no means of reality-testing, we cannot tell whether this monster is fantastic or real. It could be, as Peter Wright's memoirs, *Spycatcher*(1987), suggest, that this state is itself so paranoid that it even perceives the 'unarmed' as a threat. We are damned if we believe, and we are damned if we don't. Our English reserve encourages us to 'see things in proportion'. But perhaps it is wiser to risk being a fool than feigning wisdom.

So, what is real and what is fantasy any longer? The value of the post-modernist critique lies here; that is, in its perception that in the realm of ideology and culture we may now be moving beyond the organization of misrepresentation, of the lie, to a world where the relationship between reality and representation has been broken down together.

One of the earliest attempts to sketch the impact of mass communications upon our collective grasp on reality was Edward Relph's book *Place and Placelessness* (1976). Whilst still firmly rooted within modernist analyses of 'mass society', and to some extent èlitist and romanticist (see his analysis of 'mass tourism' for example), Relph was one of the first to discern the manner in which representations of 'place' were increasingly experienced as more 'real' than the reality to which such representations referred. Specifically, Relph outlines three trends which have become key elements in the post-modernist critique of contemporary capitalism: Disneyfication, Museumification and Futurization. According to Relph the products of Disneyfication are 'absurd, synthetic places' made up of a congelation of 'history, myth, reality and fantasy' (p. 95). The resulting representation constitutes an idealized world; one without violence, conflict, dominance or any kind of 'impurity'.[3] 'Disneyland' should be understood here purely as the prototype of a more generalized process within the leisure, tourism and retailing business within which the Disney Corporation, through contemporary mega-developments such as Orlando and Euro-Disney, is merely the exemplar.

The common element of such developments is not so much the manipulation of tastes as the engineering of experience: either the creation of a generalized 'festive' atmosphere which will then induce readiness to consume or the design of specific experiences, experiences which are themselves 'the commodity' for purchase.

The Baltimore waterfront development is an example of the former, in which all three trends that Relph discerned have been brought together in a projected $2 billion programme. The development is built upon the three 'legs' of eating and drinking, sightseeing and shopping, stimulated by a constant series of planned festivals and street entertainments. According to Terry Stevens (1988) of the Anian Group, the product constitutes 'an ever-changing scene with a dynamic range of events and a constant kaleidoscope of retailing developments' (p. 57). It is a product within which overhead walkways jostle with ornate trolley services; restored and replica clippers cram the inner marina; and the National Aquarium includes , as an exhibit, a 64 ft high Tropical Rainforest (for those of us who will be too late to catch the real thing before it disappears). Here, then, we find a collage of 'realities' ripped from their original context and relocated in a late-twentieth-century Brave New World. At the micro level of the individual site or exhibit we encounter the more specific strategy of 'designer experiences'.

The notion of thematization (themed restaurants, themed shopping stores, themed sports or heath facilities) has been an integral part of such developments, but even here trends move very quickly. Some of the earliest attempts to thematize developments – The West Edmonton Mall (Shields, 1989) and Gateshead's MetroCentre – are already considered passé by much of the business. Metroland is based upon Fantasyland One of the West Edmonton complex; its theme is the enchanted kingdom of King Wiz who rules with the help of his courtiers: Practical Joker, Whimsey the Dragon and Captain Swashbuckle. It cost over £10 million to build (small by Disney standards but large for the UK) and presents a large, fixed site providing a range of rides, displays and entertainments. The problem with such developments lies in the unvarying and standardized nature of the extravaganza provided. According to Harold Silverman (1988, p. 45) of Marketplace Design, the Edmonton concept 'merely recreates themes with boring regularity', it lacks spontaneity and the capacity to provide a changing vista over time, its 'uniform marble, chrome and terrazzo will date and fade, gradually losing the capacity to attract people out of town'. Silverman sees the Horton Plaza in San Diego as the exemplar of future developments: 'an organic, dynamic construction that allows free move- ment and change' by encouraging retailers to be as original in their shop design as the individuality [*sic*] of their surroundings. He goes on, breath- lessly:

> Tenants have taken the cue enthusiastically and have produced a won- derful, often amusing, array of high-quality fascias and interiors. Outside one cookie shop, a giant nozzle emits irresistible smells of freshly baked goodies. Meanwhile on a chip shop fascia, giant polystyrene chips jut out at crazy angles. Nearby, a toy shop sports a large fibre-optics sign that constantly changes form and colour. Far from appearing disparate or kitsch, this riot of imagination provides a visual whole far more effective than the blandness of West Edmonton. (pp. 45–6)

This fusion of building and spectacle, of design and retailing, of gadgetry and commerce, of popular culture, science, technology and entertainment is given the name 'imagineering' in the trade. Its effect is much like that achieved by pressing the button of a television set: the product bombards the senses with an immediacy of stimulation (in this case 'olfactory' besides aural and visual) compared to which the everyday reality of 'wake-break- fast-travel-work-travel-home-sleep' seems shadowy and insubstantial.

Baudrillard (1983) speaks of such sites as a form of 'hyper-reality' and, though he naively exaggerates the pervasiveness of the hyper-real (produc- ing a post-modern variant upon the old Marcusian theme of the totally administered society), the real value of this analysis nevertheless emerges when such developments are situated in the context of the post-Hiroshima secret state. How can we get our minds around these juxtapositions of the late twentieth century: of the Baltimore Waterfront, McDonalds, the Amazon Forests and the National Aquarium; of San Diego, the centre of the USA 'death industry' (defence manufacturing) and the Horton Plaza; of Fantasyland and the neglected wastes of Tyneside? Reason seems to fail us here, we try to grasp the opposing images but it is so hard, it is so much easier to embrace the immediate, the idealized, the fascinating world of the image. After all, there is just a chance that these are 'bombs for peace', that this hole in the ozone layer will go away, that the forests will grow again, that real jobs will return to Gateshead. The question, then, is not only 'What is real and what is fantasy?; *the* issue, and it is the only one that can guide us through our confusional states, is 'What do you want to be real, what do you have the courage to see as real, and what do you want as fantasy?'

When Klein first developed the notion of symbolic equivalence, she had in mind the process by which words, objects and images lose their symbolic value and become 'things in themselves'. She saw this as a psychically generated process corresponding to a state of internal catastrophe. What I have endeavoured to illustrate is the way in which the form of late-capitalist culture creates an external reality which induces a state of mind analogous to a form of internal collapse; a state in which the essential subjective process of reality testing is actively undermined.

In conclusion, then, I hope I have managed to convey the value of the psychoanalytic notion of 'state of mind' for an understanding of everyday life in the contemporary world. Considered phenomenologically, Klein's 'positions' provide us with the means with which to consider the relationship between two fundamental forms of selfhood: the self-as-object or, as I have put it, the state of 'it-ness', and the self-as-subject. The development of subjectivity (the achievement of the depressive position) is always a matter of 'more-or-less', even when viewed from the perspective of orthodox psychoanalysis – a perspective within which real, constitutive external reality is largely absent. I have tried to demonstrate that when we let external reality into this perspective the task of securing a properly subjective state of mind becomes a process of unceasing struggle. As subjects we are constantly confronted by both an internal and external establishment for whom the 'good subject' is one full of facts but without a thought in his or her head.

NOTES

1 Interestingly enough, the most detailed statement of that object-relational position which rejects the possibility of an original state of primary narcissism comes from one of Klein's closest collaborators, Paula Heimann (1952).

2 Despite some obvious shortcomings in her work, such as the tendency to have an idealized picture of the child, Alice Miller's (1988) work constitutes an important statement of the actual violence (physical and emotional) carried out by parents on their children. It is all too easy for psychoanalysis to dismiss the vital message Miller seeks to convey by characterizing her work as idealized, eclectic or lacking in rigour.

3 I remember watching a video of Tom Peters, a leading American business consultant, waxing on about excellent US companies. The Disney Corporation were extolled for the seriousness with which they practised 'customer care', the empirical proof of which, Peters croaked, was the impossibility of finding any litter on Disney premises.

6

The Institutionalization of Shallowness

The city of Bristol lies at the westernmost end of what has become termed 'the M4 (Motorway) corridor', a region lying largely within the Thames and Avon basins and one of the major growth points within the British economy. In many ways Bristol is a beautiful and prosperous city in which to live, but this very congeniality masks something quite rotten and corrupting. An alternative description of the M4 corridor, one used by some academic colleagues of mine who have done detailed research on the productive base of this region, would be 'Death Valley'. Indeed, dependency on what we euphemistically call 'defence industries' is particularly great in the Bristol area, with British Aerospace, Digital Electronics, Dowty and GEC Avionics being a few of the many industries around here engaged in the 'attack business'.

Living in the north of the city, I find many of my friends and neighbours are employed by those companies. Like me, they are middle-class, educated types with a progressive attitude towards many public issues: they didn't vote for Thatcher; they're concerned about the environment; many are also against 'the bomb'; but they work in industries which not only have no value but which are destructive of value. They are a glaring example of a much wider problem; other contemporaries of mine work in retailing, land development and life insurance. Why do they do what they do? Why do people who have a strong sense of moral value and purpose in other aspects of their life waste their working lives away in activities which have only the most tenuous moral purpose? Well, clearly, money helps. It helps accommodate once lively minds to practical problems. But if the issue was just one of 'accommodation' it would be easy to understand. Perhaps these contemporaries of mine were conscious of making an accommodation at some point in the past. The fact is, however, that many are now deeply attached to the companies they work for. I use the word 'attached' advisedly. We tend to think of attachment in terms of a positive, loving bond. Here, however, I'm using it to refer to the tying of two things together, to their fixedness, glued-togetherness. What might the nature of this attachment be?

What follows is an exploration of the organizational experience of those who work by brain in managerial, professional, technical and scientific occupations: 'educated types' whose business it is to think but not to think too much. It is an attempt to examine how the eclipse of moral and aesthetic values by technical values contributes to a lack of dimensionality in organizational settings, manifest in a subtle but pervasive sense of 'flatness'; a sense that, despite one's attachment to the place, there's 'something missing'. Above all, how might we understand the psychodynamics of groups and institutions in which the 'why of things' has become flattened by the 'how of things'; that is, in which questions of value have become split off and dissociated from questions of technique?

THE INSTRUMENTAL ATTITUDE

The triumph of technique over purpose, though implicit in the whole of Marx's project, was articulated and examined most thoroughly by Max Weber (1978) in his exploration of the difference between substantive and purposive rationality. The Frankfurt School in turn, through an appropriation of Weber's work, developed a critique of modern life as a mode of existence dominated by its instrumentality.

For Weber the development of industrial capitalism was accompanied by the secularization of life – the encroachment of a 'scientific' and calculative means–ends rationality into economy, state and civil society. In Habermas's recent formulation (1986) an original, pre-industrialized and largely undifferentiated life world contained within it a proximate equilibrium between three modes of existence, defined in terms of our relations to the external world, to others and to the inner world of subjectivity. Each mode of relatedness corresponds to a form of rationality: purposive-rational, normative (moral) and expressive (aesthetic). Industrial capitalism, however, privileged only the first mode of relatedness and its attendant form of rationality, thus producing a progressive eclipse of moral and aesthetic, as opposed to technical, meanings. Weber coined the term 'disenchantment' to express his sense of the impact of this eclipse upon the modern world. This privileged rationality then becomes split off from moral and aesthetic value, and in this sense the issue of 'ends' ('for what purpose?') becomes drained of human significance; purposive rationality becomes *rationality without purpose*, in other words, instrumental reason. As such it can be counterposed to 'substantive rationality' in which technical, moral and aesthetic value remains integrated. The point is that the development of 'technique', that is, of society's productive forces, is not necessarily equivalent to the triumph of instrumental rationality. Only where the development of technique, as with capitalism, is tied to a developmental logic (of the expanded reproduction of capital) beyond human purpose, is this triumph ensured. If the term 'socialism' still has any emancipatory meanings it must stand for the reappropriation of technique by human purpose, the replacement of production for production's sake by production for human need; that is, by socially useful production.

What justification is there for talking of the dominance of 'production for production's sake'? An example may help here. The Canary Wharf development on the Isle of Dogs in London's East End is the largest of its kind in Western Europe. When completed, its centrepiece will consist of an office tower 200 feet taller than the tallest office block (London's NatWest building) in Europe. Current development estimates stand at £4.7 billion and it is reckoned it will draw 57,000 jobs to the Isle of Dogs (though pitifully few of these will go to local people). Once completed, it will have such an enormous impact on land values in the area that all analysts agree it will unleash a new wave of development in the surrounding area. The implication of this is that many of the smaller residential, commercial and retail developments taking place on the island, developments preceding Canary Wharf and associated with the 'yuppification' of the East End in the 1980s, are already obsolete. Indeed, redevelopment plans already exist for developments which are still not fully completed! Here then is capital with its leash off, engaged in a process of constant destruction, reconstruction and renewed destruction. It is a process dictated by the nature of capital as a phenomenon which can exist only by reproducing itself in an expanded form. In this sense capital cannot rest; the principle is, 'If you've got it, then put it to work'; idle capital dissolves in one's hands. Marx's whole analysis of the accumulation of capital is an analysis of the paramountcy of production, of a society where consumption occurs for production's sake, as a prop and support for a production process trapped in its own restless logic. Much of the history of the twentieth century is the history of the development of technologies – mass communications, advertising, credit, retailing – for harnessing consumption to production. As a result we are constantly confronted by a myriad commodities, each of which insinuates itself upon us, beckons us towards it.

Returning now to the notion of instrumentality, it is possible to examine its effectiveness at a number of different levels. First, it means that the world, considered in both its natural and human forms, has no value in itself; rather, its only value lies in its being 'put to work' as an instrument in the restless process of production: the 'being of things' is eclipsed by the 'doing of things'. Indeed, arguably, this attitude has found expression in the individual's attitude towards him or herself. A friend of mine, recently returned from the USA, remarked on the perplexity she felt in experiencing the exhausting weekend leisure routine of her American hosts, a ceaseless round of activities geared to body maintenance and the accumulation of new skills and experiences and an attitude towards the self which perceives no value in leaving it to be, only in putting it 'to use'.

At another level, instrumentality refers to how things are done, that is, to 'the manner of doing'. It is the process by which 'means' are judged not in themselves, as things in themselves to which value judgements might be applied, but only in terms of their efficacy (Benjamin, 1978, pp. 35–7) – ultimately their efficacy in terms of the extent to which they serve the requirements of the firm. Take fast-food retailing as an example. The lovable clown who invited our children to consume his burgers served to conceal a quite different reality: the destruction of the Amazon forests made way for the cattle ranches that provided the company's beef. One can add to this the company's complicity in the destruction of the ozone layer through the use of CFCs in the construction of the cartons and containers in which the beef was served. The point is that companies make judgements concerning how things are done only if they serve the requirements of competition. Companies do switch to more environment-friendly means of production if failure to do so would place them at a competitive disadvantage. But the criterion for judging those means still remains that of efficacy.

Finally, instrumentality comes to mediate the individual's attitude to work. The individual's orientation becomes necessarily utilitarian and calculative. By now we all know of individuals who have suffered the consequence of misplaced loyalty; people who have given the best years of their life to an organization to whom they are now dispensable. People learn not to build up their hopes, not to lose their sense of perspective. The greatest danger is to feel successful and appreciated, for when the blow comes it falls hardest on those least anticipating it. The problem is that, despite ourselves, we do get attached to the organizations in which we spend our lives, notwithstanding their instrumentality. And it is to an examination of the nature of this attachment, and specifically the way in which organizational forms bind and entrap organizational participants, that we must now turn.

BUREAUCRATIZATION AND BEYOND

At the time when Weber was developing this notion of instrumental rationality, the emerging predominant form through which the organization of production was achieved corresponded to the classical bureaucracy of the German state. At that time 'bureaucracy' was a form very much congruent with the developing organizational requirements of a factory system in which control had become detached from ownership and in which the first stirrings of the new mass-production technologies could be discerned. The bureaucratization of industrial organizations was mediated through the work of early management theorists like Fayol (1916). With hindsight, it is now possible to see how this particular organizational form, rather than being universally applicable to industrial capitalism as Weber implied, was actually fundamental to the development of a particular form of the capitalist mode of production, namely, that associated with the diffusion of Fordist mass-production techniques.

Weber confused instrumental rationality with the organizational form, bureaucratized mass production, in which it first emerged. Today the bureaucratic form is in decline because of its lack of fit with the newly emergent productive technologies such as robotics and Information Technology (IT). The new private companies are organized on altogether different principles from bureaucratic ones, even though their instrumentalism remains unquestionable. Similarly, the form of the state is undergoing a radical transformation: in Britain, the monolithic bureaucracy that was the Civil Service is being broken up into semi-autonomous agencies; throughout Europe, city government is undergoing a process of radical decentralization, and so on. We live increasingly in a post-bureaucratic world. The task of analysis is to examine how these two dominant organizational forms have provided different means of binding individuals to institutions within which the value dimension has become split off and dissociated.

To compare Fordism with post-Fordism is to compare two completely different generative principles of production. Based upon maximum use of mass-production technologies, Fordism gave primacy to economies of scale. It was the era of company 'giantism', of the huge industrial bureaucracies which sought control over the labour process through hierarchy, rountinization and surveillance. On the other hand, post-Fordism, based upon the development of more customized production technologies, gives primacy to economies of scope or flexibility. Operational control is exercised primarily through contract rather than through hierarchy and, whilst production often becomes radically decentralized, strategic control tends to become ever more highly centralized and invisible (a kind of remote control). I wish to demonstrate that these differing principles made for quite different modes of employee involvement, underpinned by quite different organizational psychodynamics. To anticipate, I would argue that mass-production bureaucracies organized regimes of passive employee consent in which bureaucratic formality represented an unconscious mode of group binding: the creation of a thick-skinned, skeletal and inertial collective body. Post-bureaucratic forms seek to create organized regimes of active employee commitment in which a simulated moral community represents a quite different mode of group binding: adhesive identification to a designed organizational interior, glitzy and ambient.

But this is to anticipate. First we must examine the regimes of consent and commitment relevant to bureaucratic and post-bureaucratic forms.

FROM 'EQUANIMITY' TO 'COMMITMENT': MODES OF ORGANIZING CONSENT

One of the classic analyses of the bureaucratic organizational form is Etzioni's *A Comparative Analysis of Complex Organizations,* first published in 1961, arguably in the heyday of Fordism in the USA. Etzioni's primary focus is an examination of the nature of the attachment or involvement of organizational participants.

Etzioni (p. 9) suggests we think in terms of a continuum of involvement from negative involvement, which he terms 'alienation', through to positive involvement, which he calls 'commitment'. Thinking of this in terms of the form of attachment of one object to another, alienation refers to a situation in which one object has to be bound or tied to another in order to prevent its 'falling away'; 'commitment' refers to a situation in which one object embraces another towards which it experiences attraction. Interestingly enough, Etzioni seems to be aware that the categories of involvement he is constructing have a broader relevance than simply the dynamics of organizations. As he notes: 'This classification of involvement can be applied to the orientation of actors in all social units and to all kinds of objects' (p. 10). In other words, he is trying to develop a classification of object-cathexes. Referring again to this continuum of involvement, Etzioni suggests three essential orientations exist between an individual and an (organizational) object: 'alienative', standing for strong negative cathexes; 'moral', standing for strongly positive cathexes; and 'calculative', standing for cathexes which are neither positive nor negative. Whilst one might question Etzioni's equation of alienating organizational regimes with the use of direct coercion,[1] of more immediate value is his analysis of calculative and moral forms of organizational attachment, for it is through these categories that he seeks to examine the organizational experience of 'workers by brain': specifically, white-collar and professional workers. Etzioni suggests that whereas the predominant form of attachment of white-collar non-professional workers is 'calculative', the predominant form for professional workers is 'moral'. However, when he examines the experience of professionals in detail it becomes clear that nearly all the examples he uses relate to professional occupations outside industry: in education, welfare services and research institutes. Subsequent analyses of professional labour make this distinction much more clearly. In particular, we might note that one of the definitive analyses of the 1970s, Terry Johnson's study *Professions and Power* (1972), suggests that professional occupations contained within commercial institutions assume a far more subordinate position than those professions which have maintained their independence from systems of corporate patronage.

With this in mind I feel we can legitimately conclude that the dominant organizational cathexis of educated labour (white-collar, technical, professional) in the context of mass-production industrial bureaucracies is 'calculative' rather than 'moral'. Etzioni calls such organizational regimes 'utilitarian'; again we might ponder the connotations this description evokes, specifically its 'instrumentalism'. The problem, then, for Fordist mass-production bureaucracies was their inability to develop a positive organizational cathexis within educated labour; rather, the predominant cathexis was one we might best describe as 'equanimity' or 'passive consent'. Clearly the tendency to routinize educated labour within such corporations worked against the development of more positive attachments, as did the tendency towards segmentalism (Moss Kanter, 1985), a tendency which encouraged the development of divisional as opposed to corporate loyalty. But in another sense equanimity as a mode of attachment was quite congruent with the requirements of mass-production regimes. Fordism was based upon the principle of standardization, that is, of large production runs of a few standard products. Economies of scale were at a premium, hence competitive advantage was obtained through economy and efficiency, not by virtue of innovation or product quality. So long as the market environment was stable – and the creation of cartels and monopolies was a corporate technique of engineering such stability (Baron and Sweezey, 1966) – the inflexibility of Fordist bureaucracies was a source of strength. All this is another way of saying that, compared with the emerging corporate regimes of today, Fordism did not demand a great deal from educated labour, other than its loyalty.

In this light the concept of 'bureaucratic mindlessness' takes on a new meaning. Robert Merton, in his study of the 'bureaucratic personality' (1957), made much use of Veblen's concept of 'trained incapacity'. By being socialized into the performance of routinized and repetitive tasks, the bureaucratic personality develops a tendency to apply a few basic principles and responses to all environmental contexts. In other words, such personalities and the regimes that they inhabit become contextually stupid. Later, Gregory Bateson (1973) was to refer to such patterns of behaviour as 'level 1' learning, equivalent to the development of a relatively fixed response to a given, stable context. However, if context changes, then the mode of responding becomes inappropriate: the individual or organization may, painfully, learn to develop a new response. In such a fashion a repertoire of responses may be developed together with the intelligence to match responses to contexts. Bateson refers to this as 'level 2' learning. It refers to a situation in which the individual or organization has acquired a certain flexibility and responsiveness without being creative. Responses and contexts are drawn from pre-existing experience. There is no internalized capacity to imagine new response–context relationships; the subject remains dependent on precedent and remains relatively helpless when faced with the unprecedented. It may become an 'early adopter' of a new technique, but it does not have the capacity to innovate. It is imitative without being innovative. Bateson's 'level 3' or 'meta-learning' refers to the capacity to innovate.

We can see then why Bateson's theories of animal and human learning have had such a profound impact on the theory of management over the last decade, for the dominant mode of organizational learning manifested by Fordist bureaucracies was completely unsuited to the emerging key principle, 'flexible adaptation', of the post-Fordist period. The very term, the Permanent Innovation Economy, that some writers (Morris Suzuki, 1984, 1986) have used to characterize the new corporate environment indicates that, without the capacity to innovate or at least imitate, the modern business organization stands little chance of survival. In other words, the emerging post-bureaucractic forms demand far more from educated labour. Loyalty and equanimity are no longer sufficient; in modern management jargon the key management task is now 'human resource development'. In terms of participants' organizational cathexis we see a shift from regimes of passive consent to the construction of regimes conducive to active commitment. The essential problem becomes how to create active commitment in organizations without substantive purpose or, in Etzioni's terms, how to induce a sense of moral involvement within organizations where substantive values are necessarily entirely subordinate.

BINDING PROCESSES IN GROUPS AND ORGANIZATIONS

At this point I wish to take a step back from the analysis which has so far been pursued. Mainstream forms of organizational analysis, as expressed by Etzioni, take us so far but they remain trapped at the surface level of administrative structure, they do not provide us with much insight into what might be termed the 'deep structure' of group and organizational life. Two alternative traditions of analysis can take us further here. The first, strongly influenced by Marxist ideas, seeks to understand organizations in terms of their levels of structure (Clegg, 1981). For example, Benson (1982) has proposed we consider three levels of organizational functioning. The first, and most superficial, he describes in terms of 'administrative structure', that is, the level of the perceptible form understood in terms of hierarchy, horizontal and vertical division of labour, explicit policy and procedures, formal job descriptions and allocation of responsibility. The second level, less perceptible, he argues, is governed by rules of interest-group formation. It constitutes a method of understanding the dynamic-through-time of organizations in terms of conflicts between managerialism and professionalism, production managers and marketing managers, intra- and interorganizational coalitions, blocs and gangs, and so on. From this perspective, organizations can be seen very much as political systems within which a range of power struggles are enacted through time. The third level of organizational functioning, Benson argues, is governed by 'rules of structure formation' which we might picture in a manner analogous to Chomsky's generative rules of grammar. Such rules, then, generate the grammar of organizations, they set the boundaries or the frame within which organizational life can occur. Within the context of the commercial firm, rules of structure formation are defined by the nature of capital, its restless and unceasing propensity towards expanded reproduction and the logic of instrumental efficacy to which it gives rise. As we shall see later, in the context of the Welfare State the rules of structure formation are quite different, being fundamentally self-contradictory, as befits an apparatus which attempts to represent the needs of both capital and labour without meeting either set of requirements effectively.

A second tradition also exists, which attempts to examine group and organizational deep structure. Whereas the Marxist tradition beholds organizations primarily as power systems, the group-psychoanalytic tradition is concerned to uncover organizations' depth when considered as human systems. Clearly, in this essay I am endeavouring to bring these two traditions together so that we might grasp the interpenetration of social with psychological deep structure as manifest in modern institutional settings. I leave the reader to judge whether the resulting marriage is voluntary or shot-gun.

How then might the group psychoanalytic tradition help us to understand the attachment of educated labour to instrumental organizational regimes? The formative study within this tradition has been Bion's early work *Experiences in Groups* (1961). At first sight this work, based as it is upon Bion's reflections on the functioning of small groups operating in a therapeutic and rehabilitative setting, seems quite inadequate to grasp the complexities of life in large institutions. Indeed, at a later point I will take to task the Tavistock Group Relations school for their failure to appropriate Bion's insights in a critical manner. The main problem with Bion's study concerns the poverty of his analysis of non-pathological modes of group functioning: compared with the detailed examination of pathological Basic Assumption Group activity he provides very little discussion of the non-pathological co-operative 'Work Group' (Brown, 1985). What I wish to do here is to extend Bion's tentative analysis of the co-operative Work Group by incorporating some of his later insights on the 'container–contained' relationship (Bion, 1962) and Bick's work on the 'skin container' function (Bick, 1968, 1986).

The essential condition for Work Group activity is, according to Bion, the existence of common purpose. In Experiences in Groups Bion doesn't take us much further than this. As Meltzer argues (1978), all of Bion's subsequent work is as applicable to our understanding of the life of the group as it is to our understanding of the development of the individual psyche, the problem being that, with a few exceptions such as Attention and Interpretation (1970), the group exists only as a subterranean background reference point in his later studies. Central to Bion's subsequent theorization, however, is the concept of the 'container–contained' relationship which, as I have argued in Chapter 4, is the prism through which Bion attempts to understand how psychical development proceeds from an initial dependence on the 'auxiliary ego' of the nurturing figure to the internalization of this capacity which is initially contained by the 'one who cares'.

Extending this notion of 'containment', Bick (1968) suggests that in its earliest form parts of the personality are felt to have 'no binding force'. The infant exists in a largely unintegrated state and must be held together in a way which is experienced passively, 'by the skin functioning as a boundary' (p. 484). But, following Bion, this internal function of containing or holding together must be conceived of as being at first derivative, 'dependent initially on the introjection of an external object, experienced as capable of fulfilling this function' (p. 484). (We might think of this external object as the containing embrace of the nurturing figure experienced in its continuity and reliability over time.) In other words, the nurturing embrace constitutes the first experience of secure boundedness, an experience which, upon incorporation, finds representation in the idea of one's own skin functioning as a boundary – Freud's corporeal ego (1923). The body of the subject is therefore itself a re-presentation of the embrace of the one who cares (in religious terms, of 'the body of Christ').

Shifting back to the group we can see how the common purpose (or in Tavistock parlance, the 'primary task') performs the same binding function as Bick's 'containing object', holding its parts together in a way whereby an integrated group emerges from a previously unintegrated seriality. The primary task, therefore, appears to perform a binding function; it acts as a container within which the group-as-subject can come together. We might think of the terms unintegration, integration and disintegration as applying equally to the constitution of the group as to the constitution of the personality. According to Bick (1968), the personality exists at first in an unintegrated state; it has no internal means of binding itself together:

> The need for a containing object would seem in the infantile uninte-grated state, to produce a frantic search for an object – a light, a voice, a smell, or other sensual object – which can hold the attention and thereby be experienced momentarily at least, as holding parts of the personality together. The optimal object is a nipple in the mouth, together with the holding and talking and familiar-smelling mother. (p. 484)

Drawing on Freud's notion that the ego must be at first a corporeal ego, Bick feels this 'optimal object' must perform a function akin to 'a skin' in which the infant and its parts (impulses, fantasies, sensations) can find some sense of enclosure and boundedness. She adds, 'disturbance in the primal skin function can lead to the development of a 'second-skin' formation' (p. 484).

Second-skin formations are essentially simulations rather than repre-sentations, they constitute a desperate attempt to simulate what cannot be represented by virtue of its never having been adequately experienced. They are thus forms of pseudo-independence in which things (Tustin's autistic objects), talents, preoccupations and even parts of the body are used as ways of holding the personality together. In a later article Bick provides a vivid example of such phenomena at work in her account of an analysis of a six-year-old girl, Sonia:

> Her last move at the end of each session was to go to the sink. There she lay on the sink, put her mouth round the tap and filled her mouth with water. She held the water until her mother came into sight as she

approached the waiting-room, whereupon she swallowed the water and held on to the mother with her eyes. The number of mouthfuls she took was proportionate to the duration of separation before weekends and holidays. There was also a phenomenon of turning cartwheels in which she was very skilful, and very ritualised skipping games with which she usually ended the session. I think that these were attempts at muscular hyperkinetic self-containment – second skin formation – when she stood before the gap. (Bick, 1986, p. 294) [The 'gap' here being her experience of separation as a hole in her going-on-being.]

In terms of the individual psyche, failure of primary or second-skin formation leads to collapse of the personality into a disintegrated state in which persecutory anxiety dominates (a consequence of the absence of any kind of protective shield). This would account for Tustin's (1986) remarks concerning the treatment of autistic children, namely, that progress from a position of simulated containment based upon the use of autistic shapes and · objects can occur only if the subject can be held through a process of controlled regression where psychotic organization dominates in order to emerge into a properly integrated, non-simulated state. Bion's suggestion appears to be that in the absence of a primary task (primary skin function) the group also collapses into a disintegrative state characterized by pre-subjective modes of Basic Assumption activity. What Bion's schema fails to provide for is any group equivalent to Bick's idea of a simulated containment.

We will return to this issue shortly, but for now we must turn our attention to how another aspect of Bick's work may help us carry our understanding of Bion's group psychology still further. Bick's second paper (1986) makes clear an issue which is partially obscured in her earlier piece, that is, the existence of 'impaired skin formations' alongside primary and simulated ones. In this case experience of the nurturing figure's work of containment is just sufficient to prevent recourse to simulation but, whilst the experience is 'real' it is also damaged or impaired. As a result, representation of this experience assumes the form of a disfigured body ego in which the containing skin is experienced as too tight, loose, full of holes, thick or thin, etc. Through such insights analysts such as Bick and Meltzer *et al.* (1986) have begun to examine the psychological meaning of a variety of disorders of the body configuration and of skin disorders such as eczema. Bick's analysis of Mary, 'she came in hunched, stiff-jointed, grotesque like a "sack of potatoes" as she later called herself' (1968, p. 485) and Szekacs'

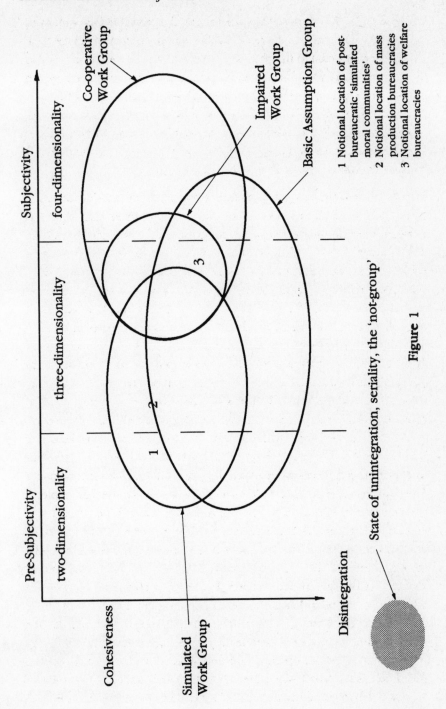

Figure 1

(1985) analysis of Helen fall within this category. Again we might ponder the application of this notion of impaired skin formations to the study of group life.

As a consequence of this discussion I would propose the schema in Figure 1 as one equally applicable to either the study of the individual or the collective psyche. In this diagram I have attempted to integrate Meltzer's notions of dimensionality in psychic life with the previous discussion of modes of psychical containment. The diagram is clearly arbitrary in many respects, but what I have tried to preserve is a notion of the interpenetration of these various collective states of being. Clearly Bion's area of Basic Assumption activity would appear to bear much in common with Klein's paranoid-schizoid position, whereas his Work Group appears to correspond to the achievements of the depressive position in group life. My suggestion is, as I hope to illustrate through an examination of the psychodynamics of welfare bureaucracy, that the impaired Work Group achieves a degree of integration but is strongly influenced by basic assumption activity. The simulated Work Group, on the other hand, appears to achieve quite a high degree of cohesiveness but I have deliberately avoided the term 'integration' here. I am therefore specifically attempting to contrast the bonding of the Work Group, real, sensuous integration brought about by the synthesis of individual desires, to the cohesiveness of the simulated Work Group which is more the result of forced congelation or agglomeration through which a 'synthesis' is engineered.

I would now like to give further meaning to the notion of dimensionality in psychical function by sketching the forms of identification common to each level. This is particularly important, given that the concept of identification may provide a more depth-psychological analysis of the phenomenon of organizational involvement Etzioni (1961) describes in terms of alienative, calculative and moral orientations.

According to Meltzer *et al.* (1975) we might think of a series of forms of identification, each of which signifies a higher level of developmental maturity. The first and most 'primitive' is the level of Freud's primary identification corresponding to a state of undifferentiation between subject and object. The second level, *adhesive identification*, corresponds to a form of differentiation-without-interiority. In other words, there is an awareness of external boundaries but not of enclosed space or place. This is a two-dimensional world. The boundaries are not containing boundaries in which psychical content can be placed, they are surfaces without depth, skins which do not yet enclose a body or a self; surfaces which when torn or ruptured lead to a falling into limitless space, into chaos. The third level, that of *projective identification* and three-dimensionality, implies not only a boundary but a boundary which can contain and receive. An enclosed space exists, albeit a phantasmic one. This would appear to be the level of functioning of Bion's Basic Assumption Groups. Consider, for example, the dependency group. Because the leader of such a group contains the projective identifications of the members, the paradox appears of a leader so powerful that he or she may resemble a deity but a deity nevertheless completely in the thrall of the group's members. In organizational life this paradox finds expression in the experience of leadership, in other words the intense pressure (at times terrifying) of expectation coming from below. We might speak of 'leaders and led', but who has the power, the leader or the led? In projective identification, psychical content is not just placed in another; pressure is exerted on this object to contain, without modification, that which has been put there. The recipient of such identifications feels coerced, in the hands of an alien force. Bion (1957b) made the important point that it is not just psychical qualities, such as strength or badness, which can be projected but mental functions themselves. For example, one of the striking features of the *dependency group* is the way in which the dependency leader becomes the container of the group's mind. One surely can explain the complete loss of normal mental faculties (judgement, discrimination, initiative, imagination) within dependency-group members only through the idea that if they have indeed 'lost their minds', then they must have placed them somewhere (within the personified leader, 'the group/party/organization', 'the Bible'). The leaders become the source of all truth, their words become enigmatic, they carry a weight, a solidity that others lack. In political parties where the dependency leader contains these abandoned minds, followers feel close to this figure despite her power, it seems that she really does 'feel what we feel and think what we think', indeed 'she takes the words right out of our mouths'.

The final, and highest, form of identification is *introjective*. It is only at this point that we can properly speak of the group leader as a collective ego-ideal. This appears to be Freud's focus in his work *Group Psychology and the Analysis of the Ego* (1921). Here the object is not just a bundle of exported projections but a real object engaged in some form of dialogue. Psychical contents and functions are now not just subject to export but to import as well; in this sense, full 'trading' between subject and object takes place. Within the dependency group the leader's strength is inversely related to the followers' weakness but, where the relation between leader and followers is based upon introjective identification, the followers are able to introject the real or fantasized strengths of the leader; hence, they can become 'little big men'. The contrast between this and adhesive identification is striking, for in this instance no psychical trading between subject and object occurs at all. The object, for instance 'the organization', does not therefore constitute an ideal. Rather, it is simply an image, a simulacrum which fascinates and holds the attention. This takes us back to Bick's idea of the substitute object, 'a light, a voice, a smell, or other sensual object – which can hold the attention and thereby be experienced momentarily at least as holding parts of the personality together' (1968, p. 484). I also suspect that we are on the same terrain as Baudrillard (1983) when he speaks of the way in which objects of consumption such as the car have lost their capacity to act as containers of psychical content. But whereas he implies that, in this sense, the consumer is no longer capable of enjoying any form of object-relationship to objects of desire, it seems to me that an object–relationship still exists but of a most primitive form; that is, it is two-dimensional.

We are now ready to return to the study of institutions and the question we posed at the end of the previous section: how can psychoanalytic group psychology facilitate our understanding of both bureaucratic equanimity and the regimes of active participant commitment established within the post-bureaucratic firm?

BUREAUCRATIC EQUANIMITY

When considering such terms as 'bureaucratic inertia' or 'bureaucratic inflexibility', we are reminded of the way in which, in everyday language, this particular organizational form is viewed as being monolithic and has become wrapped up in connotations of denseness and impenetrability.

As we have noted before, Weber (1978) believed that bureaucracy was the necessary mode of insertion of 'rationality without purpose' into organizational life. The manner by which authority became invested in 'impersonal order' seemed entirely congruent with the idea that bureaucracy be considered modern: for 'authority', at least, progress seemed to have arrived once its work could be concealed within the rational ordering of things. But whereas Weber merely sought to describe 'bureaucratic order', others, like Fayol, sought to prescribe it. Among Fayol's (1916) principles of administration can be found ideas such as the advocacy of the rational division of functions within ordered hierarchies, the unity of command, and firm and consistent discipline. In particular, proponents of bureaucratic modernization stressed attention to the rational design of the formal administrative structure; functional specialization; unitary and hierarchical command structures; the precise specification of duties and responsibilities; the creation of a comprehensive and impersonal body of rules and procedures; clearly delineated career advancement ladders; and so on. As a result, a set of binary oppositions came to dominate organizational thinking in the bureaucratic era, such as the opposition between 'formal' and 'informal' organization; between 'task' and 'socio-emotional' activity; between 'rational' and 'irrational' organizational behaviour; and so on. One can see here, in the background, the crowd, the dangerous class, the emotional side of things, the id, things to be tamed through the processes of discipline and normalization: as Cooper and Burrell (1988) note, rational organization becomes an embodiment of Foucault's regime of 'disciplinary technology'. Bureaucracy, then, comes to represent an impersonal super-ego whose task it is to keep impulse in check through regimentation and routinization. Only later, with the decline of Fordism, do such impulses become reconstrued as human resources to be tapped rather than as dirt in the machine to be ground down and flushed away.

This line of analysis focusing upon bureaucratic authority, that is, the depersonalization of authority into rational order, was the dominant theme within the Frankfurt School's critique of bureaucratic modernity. I feel Jessica Benjamin (1978) is probably justified in drawing the link between bureaucratization and patriarchy, as she notes: 'The original split and antagonism between the sexes in our society would thus persist through the objective, generalised denial of nurturance and the supremacy of instrumental activity. We could think of this as patriarchy without the father' (p. 36). But the psychoanalytic insights which have informed this critique drew (necessarily, given the Germanic culture within which they were developed) upon the classical corpus of the psychoanalytic tradition and specifically upon Freud's structural theory of *The Ego and the Id* (1923). The Frankfurt tradition to this day remains largely ignorant of the radical extension to the psychoanalytic paradigm constituted by the work of Klein and the post-Kleinians. Such developments, in which the work of Bion, Bick and Meltzer has played a pivotal role, provide us with the basis of an altogether different insight into the nature of bureaucratic functioning.

As should by now be clear, my contention is that within organizations, where the value dimension is necessarily split off and dissociated, no natural collective binding processes exist. I am assuming here that Bion's Work Group is roughly synonymous with Etzioni's concept of the normative organization in which moral commitment is the predominant mode of group cathexis. The absence of substantive purpose would leave the organization in a non-integrated state unless other means of binding participants psychologically to the organization could be found (let us remember at this point that our primary focus is on the experience of educated labour within organizational settings rather than the experience of manual labour). I would argue that these 'other means', whether bureaucratic or post-bureaucratic, share this essential function in common: they represent forms of simulated organizational containment.

How might we begin to understand the manner in which Fordist bureaucracies provided a form of simulated organizational containment? To pursue this line of analysis is to investigate the psychological investment of participants in bureaucracies. The first thing to note about the bureaucratic form is the way in which such regimes of routinization shield organizational participants from uncertainty. You know where you are in a bureaucracy. Monotony may seem a small price to pay within regimes designed to eradicate the unexpected and the unpredictable. Stable career progression, clearly specified areas of responsibility, simple and understandable hierarchies of authority, these and many other features of bureaucratic life combine together to create an institutional body which is solid, thick and visceral. Bureaucracy, then, constitutes a form of rigid containment within which the dominant anxiety is claustrophobic: the fear of being shut in, trapped, stuck. We speak pejoratively of people being 'stuck in a groove' or of having been 'stuck at such and such a place for umpteen years' without recognizing the way in which this very 'stuckness' is a source of both anxiety and reassurance.

At another level one is struck by the psychological investment participants have in the depersonalization and 'taskiness' of such regimes. Speaking of Bion's conditions for Work Group Organization, Meltzer notes that of these conditions the one that is most frequently missing is a task. He adds, 'this is not always apparent because real tasks and delusional tasks are not easily distinguished' (1986, p. 195). From my own work as a consultant to organizations I am convinced that the tasks with which staff busy themselves within bureaucracies, far from being 'primary', are actually an organized defence against the pain of thought. My sense is that an essential characteristic of the delusional task is the way in which it becomes construed as an end in itself, just as the Delusional Work Organization sees the 'need' for organizational survival and self-reproduction as an end in itself. In such situations the question, 'Survival for what purpose?', is potentially catastrophic. 'Dropping out' is a dangerous business; we tend to underestimate the deep sense of ontological security individuals derive from participation in bureaucratic routines (Wilmott, 1986).

It is not that bureaucracies lack depth or, in this sense, are superficial. Quite the contrary, they are very dense and visceral structures. One senses, however, that the bureaucratic relationship with reality is in many ways quite paranoid: bureaucracies deal with the environment by attempting to control it (hence the classical strategies of monopoly control, price-fixing cartels, etc). In the propitious market environment of the 1950s and 1960s, powerful Fordist bureaucracies were able to control the environment in this way with great success. The sudden emergence of the OPEC oil-producing nations in the early 1970s, however, heralded an era of market turbulence in which such strategies broke down. It is as if the giant industrial bureaucracies of the post-war boom period could not tolerate this idea of the market environment having a life of its own; it had itself to be subjected to bureaucratic control: ordered, regimented and standardized. When we speak of these times as the period of 'mass consumption' we often fail to examine the full implications of this term, for it was also the era of standardized culture and the standardized consumer. Vitality and unpredictability were therefore a source of threat to industrial bureaucracies, in terms of both their internal and external worlds. We can see, therefore, an element of flight in bureaucratic regimes from an unpredictable world into the ordered routines of a rigidly containing internal environment. In this context 'bigness' acquires important symbolic meaning. 'The company' becomes a highly reified phenomenon whose assumed strength, besides being a source of anomie, also provides a sense of protection. In this way bureaucratic regimes were able to mobilize basic assumption activity and put it to use for organizational survival. Specifically, we might think of bureaucracies as dependency cultures in which participants are invited to suspend their mental capacity to judge, discriminate and initiate. 'The organization' becomes a reified container for the projection of participants' mental functions; people literally lose their minds within the impersonal order of things.

The line of analysis that I am adopting here enables us to see the irrationality of bureaucratic rationality and therefore provides a means of going beyond the approach implicit within much of the work of Weber and the Frankfurt School, an approach which tends to regard such 'rationality' at face value. I am attempting to show how such regimes resort to the elaborate manipulation of structures and procedures in order to construct a simulation of organizational containment and, hence, to the creation of the experience of an internal organizational space in which participants can feel safely located. The dictionary defines a 'simulation' as 'something having merely the form or appearance of a certain thing' (*Shorter Oxford English Dictionary*). In this case the 'thing' refers to an organization bound together by a commonly understood substantive purpose, that is, a purpose in which technical, moral and ethical values remain integrated. It is the absence of such purpose within instrumental institutions which forces the recourse to simulation.

The concept of 'simulation' should be clearly distinguished from 'dissimulation'. Whereas the former relates closely to the idea of 'imitation' the latter draws much more upon the verb 'to dissemble'. According to the dictionary, the verb 'dissimulate' means 'to alter or disguise the semblance so as to deceive; to give a false semblance to'. And with this in mind we should now move on to consider the nature of the organizational regimes which have superseded bureaucracy, that is, to a study of the post-modern institution.

THE USES OF 'IRRATIONALITY'

The old rationality is, in our opinion, a direct descendant of Frederick Taylor's school of scientific management and has ceased to be a useful discipline.
(In Search of Excellence: Lessons from America's Best-Run Companies, 1982, p. 42)

This extract comes from a book by Thomas Peters and Robert Waterman (1982) which can be regarded as the key management text of the early post-Fordist era. The book is both a sustained attack on the assumptive world of the bureaucratic order and a vivid statement of the principles underlying the construction of the post-bureaucratic regime. The book (an all-time best seller in both the USA and Britain) announces a key shift in the relationship between the industrial organization and educated labour; between institutional power and human impulse. In place of the bureaucratic denigration of the informal, the irrational and the emotional we find a new managerial discourse which celebrates such things: 'good managers make meanings for people as well as money' (p. 29). In place of the bureaucratic denial of psychological reality (a denial which, as we have seen, returned to haunt the bureaucratic order), we have a new perspective in which the acceptance of psychological reality is the prelude to its full-blown manipulation. In place of the institution as the impersonal regulator of impulse we perceive the emergence of an institutionalized libidinal ego harnessing impulse to the cause of instrumental efficacy: Marcuse's 'repressive desublimation' returned to the world of work from the world of consumption.

As we have already seen, the decline of the Fordist era in the 1970s necessitated a shift from the principle of 'standardization' to that of 'flexible adaptation'. Organizational performance is no longer judged in terms of economy and efficiency but increasingly in terms of quality and innovativeness. Bureaucratic mindlessness can no longer deliver the goods. Regimes of passive organizational consent which expect little more of educated labour than its loyalty are no longer adequate in these new times. The task for the post-Fordist organization is to harness those human capacities which were neglected and routinized by the previous regimes. In Etzioni's terms the trick is to develop a positive organizational cathexis of the kind achieved in normative organizations (religious, political and voluntary) but, in this case, within institutions without substantive purpose. For this reason I feel we can talk of the strategy of the post-Fordist organization being the reconstitution of the company as a 'simulated moral community'.

Peters and Waterman unselfconsciously catalogue the psychological deficiencies of the old regimes: 'managers don't personally identify with what their companies do' (p. 35); 'caring about what you're doing is considered either unimportant or taken for granted' (p. 38); 'the rationalist approach does not celebrate informality' (p. 50); and so on. In contrast, managers within the new regimes 'create a broad, uplifting, shared culture, a coherent framework within which charged-up people search for appropriate adaptations'. They add that 'such purpose invariably emanates from love of product, providing top-quality services, and honouring inno-vation and contribution from all' (p. 51). One might wince at the idea of managers and technicians being encouraged to develop a love of product, but Peters and Waterman have no such qualms, they deliver veritable paeons of praise to executives who have declared their love for burger-buns, potato chips, etc.

In a chapter entitled 'Man waiting for motivation', these authors then proceed to draw the Achilles heel of organizational participants: 'we desperately need meaning in our lives and will sacrifice a great deal to institutions that will *provide meaning* for us' (p. 56); excellent companies teach us that we can design systems in which 'most of their people are *made to feel* that they are winners' (p. 57). Moreover they are designed 'to celebrate the winning once it occurs. . . they are full of hoop la' (p. 58). Like a couple of smiling vultures Peters and Waterman swoop in upon the frail and needy human being. Every possible psychological need provides an opportunity for exploitation. They plunder the play box of modern psycho-logy, drawing on insights from attribution theory, Zen, neuro-linguistic programming, Gregory Bateson and Bruno Bettelheim. Everything is as-sembled here, the whole box of delights; each is pulled out, scrutinized and twisted into another little hook by which to catch the unwitting employee. Here's an extract which gives a flavour of their work:

> The total of left - and right-brain research suggests simply that businesses are full (100%) of highly 'irrational' (by left-brain standards), emotional human beings: people who want desperately to be on winning teams ('seek transcendence'); individuals who thrive on the camaraderie of an effective small group or unit setting ('avoid isolation'); creatures who *want to be made to feel* that they are in at least partial control of their destinies ('fear helplessness'). (Peters and Waterman, 1982, p. 60)

A bit later we find them vandalizing the findings of cognitive dissonance research: 'only if you get people acting, even in small ways, the way you want them to, will they come to believe in what they're doing' (p. 75). Countless other examples could be given detailing their open advocacy of psychological manipulation. The point is that the very success of this evocative, racy but deeply offensive book is an expression of the sudden but profound shift which occurred in the exercise of organizational control in the 1970s: from concealment within routinized order it now finds expression through the systematic manipulation of organizational culture. Managers with their sleeves rolled up working with the boys [*sic*] on the shop floor, senior executives 'walking the job', company sweatshirts, regular plant-wide binges and celebrations, corporate 'mission statements' and logos and, at the sickest level, concern for what are euphemistically called 'corporate values' ('quality is everybody's business', 'learn from the customer', etc).

Actually, I have a feeling that post-bureaucratic strategies of control cannot be contained by the idea of systematic cultural manipulation. It strikes me that the logic of the new developments leads us towards the notion of 'the designed organizational interior', a counterpart no doubt of those wider cultural developments in which the process of commodification has gone beyond consumption to the commodification of meaning and experience itself. I am particularly struck by the correspondence between current designs for organizational living and certain developments in leisure and retailing, specifically the integration of the shopping mall and the 'leisureplex' into a kind of 'total consumer institution'. The idea is that the modern out-of-town retail and leisure complex should become a total shopping and recreational experience, not merely a functional site one goes to in order to buy commodities. Indeed, this notion of the total consumer institution has been adopted by a number of the larger stores which no longer present themselves just as a place to shop but as a self-contained and miniaturized reality. Take Children's World (a British store) as an example. Within this store mum and dad can shop or have a snack while the children are distracted by playing on modern equipment under staff supervision. Baby's bottle can be warmed, prams mended in one unit, nappies changed in another. Mothercare shows its toddler customers videos and provides them with drinks at the milk and juice bar. Everything is thought of. Planning for informality is taken to such lengths that real spontaneity disappears into the pores of its simulacrum. Every eventuality, every age-group, is catered for. In a recent article Peter Sargent of Sargent and Potiriadis (one of the leading development consultants in the leisure and retailing field) outlined his vision of the future for 'the grey power people', the silver fifties and sixties (otherwise known in the marketing business as Woopies: well-off older people). He writes:

> Shopping centres will need to develop ways to giving grey-haired people a good time for the day. Older people don't like to hurry. There

might be a premium on quieter, non-spending space and even on the inclusion of communal rooms. Imagine, two hours' bridge before shopping, then lunch followed by shopping, perhaps a film and a spa bath, then a drink and dinner and – just to finish off, some late night shopping. All in one pleasant place. (Sargent, 1988, p. 40)

Before you reach for your gun I should remind you that Peters, Waterman and Sargent may really believe in what they say; it is possible that, for them, Hewlett Packard and the West Edmonton Mall provide a glimpse of future paradise, a reality where everyone is cheerful and everyone pulls together. We might think, then, of this movement towards the painstaking design of institutional interiors as something common to work, shopping, leisure, tourist and other organizations in the post-modern era. The key term seems to me to be 'ambience', something to do with the tone, the atmosphere, the 'feel' of the place.

To return to the world of work, we therefore need to think beyond the shaping of an organizational culture to the creation of a specific organizational ambience. The new regimes have not, as Peters and Waterman imply, abandoned the use of rational planning; rather, the object of planning has shifted from systems and procedures (the 'formal' organization) to human relations themselves. The new 'human planning' strategies are as extensive as they are imperceptible; the trick is to design situations in ways which build commitment to the product. To refer back to *In Search of Excellence*, it is not that people are 'winners' but that they are 'made to feel' winners; it is not that one has to give employees any real control over their destinies, because employees are simply 'creatures who want to be made to feel' that they are in control, and so on. Here, then, we find the art of simulation taken to the highest degree: the simulation of teamwork, the simulation of enthusiasm, the simulation of caring (hoop la!) and the simulation of values. Above all, as I have suggested, we should consider the post-bureaucratic regime as a 'simulated moral community'. Etzioni's (1961) analysis is helpful again here for in his discussion of moral organizational involvement he argued that this orientation can assume two different forms: 'social commitment' and 'moral commitment'. Whereas the latter is built upon the internalization of norms and identification with legitimate authority (an essentially inner-directed orientation), 'social commitment' is based much more upon social conformity to peer group pressure (what Etzioni calls 'horizontal relationships'). The simulated moral communities of Digital and

Hewlett Packard are clearly built upon the latter principle. A casual visitor (and HP welcomes visitors with the same enthusiasm and cheerfulness that they practise on the shop floor) cannot but be struck by the way in which such companies reek of other-directed 'buddyness': 'we're all on first-name terms here'. I am reminded of Gosling's notion of the pseudo-mutual group or institution (1979).

What, then, can we say about the institutional body of such post-bureaucratic regimes? My sense is of a simulated skin where everything is primarily on the surface. There is no hidden depth here, rather an identification with a phantasmic collective excellence: idealized, glitzy and bonhomic. The organization lacks even the dimensionality of the bureaucratic form. There is no containing object, simply an image, a simulacrum, which fascinates. The primary mode of identification is therefore adhesive rather than projective or introjective. Within such settings the boundary between reality and unreality is almost entirely destroyed. After socialization into such cultures it becomes almost impossible for participants to distinguish between what is genuine and what is false: between joy and 'cheerfulness'; between solidarity and 'buddyness'; between commitment and 'enthusiasm'. One wonders, therefore, whether we should speak of dissimulation rather than simulation for it is as if such regimes constitute a systematic misrepresentation of reality.

Behind this screen of lies a different reality can be discerned, one both aggressive and cynical. The newer regimes, despite being much more decentralized, fluid and flexible than their predecessors, still require a core of organizational members geared to those routine puzzle-solving activities which dominated the stable bureaucracies of the past. But they also require a new cadre of organizational radicals owing no loyalty to precedent or routine. Kuhn's (1970) metaphor of scientific paradigms may help us here. For Kuhn, so long as a particular paradigm remains undisturbed the predominant mode of activity occurring within it is what he terms the 'routine problem-solving activity' of 'normal science'. Stable organizational regimes, the regimes of the 1950s and 1960s, were like this. But during periods, like today, when the economy goes through a process of structural transformation, normal problem-solving activities, whilst still a necessary condition, are no longer a sufficient condition for the self-reproduction of business or government organizations. In such situations organizations must revolutionize themselves or die (death may assume many forms: takeover, bankruptcy or, in the case of British local government, abolition), and to do this a new cadre of organizational members is required, capable of establishing an aggressive distance from the past. This new layer displays an active contempt for the organizational conservatives and their timorous clinging to outmoded methods and assumptions. Yet despite at one level being quite creative – the basis of the new regimes' capacity to imitate and innovate – at another level the new cadres are the harbingers of the new shallowness. This is a shallowness which knows of itself, indeed one which in private, over drinks or dinner, revels in and celebrates its shallowness. The new organizational radicals, glimpsed by Lasch (1985) through his examination of the emergent survivalist executive culture of the USA, are able to play the role required of them precisely because of their wariness of attachments of any form. Lasch notes some of the personal qualities of this new type: ironic self-observation, protean selfhood, emotional anaesthesia. Such characters are not easily taken in. To the ordinary organizational member, perhaps used to working in more bureaucratic regimes, the new companies seem different, worth working for. To the new cadres, those moving upwards in the modern corporate world, the organization is dispensable. 'Go for it' is the password, cynical self-deprecation is the preferred mode of psychological defence. Even the most vicious attempt at parody is turned by such characters into a pretext for celebration: the British comedian Harry Enfield can eat his heart out, 'Loadsamoney'[2] couldn't hurt them, indeed they have adopted this caricature as their champion. No matter how crude he is in his use of money, he cannot seem to out-caricature reality. The new cadres know that the 'community' is a lie, that behind the ambience nothing of substantive value exists. They are not expected to stay with the company for long; indeed, if they did, questions would soon be raised regarding their calibre. Such modern narcissists hardly know the meaning of commitment; they can simply move from company to company drawing upon an apparently endless vein of enthusiasm.

THE SIMULATED INSTITUTIONAL BODY

I have suggested a correspondence between Bion's concept of the Work Group and the Weberian concept of substantive rationality. It follows that an institution without substantive purpose has no natural body, there is no endogenous synthesizing force to bind its elements together. Whilst capitalist institutions have always tended to rely on forms of coercion to control manual labour, they have tended to rely on engineering consent in order to manage educated labour. I have attempted to demonstrate how bureaucratic industrial organizations constituted regimes of passive consent in which bureaucratic structures and procedures were used as the material for the construction of a simulated institutional body. Furthermore, I have suggested that bureaucracy and instrumental rationality are not equivalent. We appear to be entering a post-bureaucratic world in which instrumental rationality is no less predominant. Post-bureaucratic capitalist institutions attempt to constitute themselves as regimes of active organizational commitment resembling simulated moral communities. Lacking the dimensionality of bureaucracies, the newer organizations rely much more upon external skin surfaces to represent the institutional body. In this sense they resemble organizational mannequins, attractively attired and with an ambient interior. I have further suggested that whereas bureaucratic institutions tend straightforwardly to simulate the absent organizational body (one can be stuck in the bowels of a bureaucracy or travelling within its labyrinth of arteries) post-bureaucratic institutions tend more towards dissimulation, in terms of both how the organization's interior is designed and how its exterior is projected. Finally, it seems to me that each institutional form draws upon a different Basic Assumption activity. Whereas 'dependency cultures' predominate in bureaucratic institutions, 'messianic pairing cultures' predominate in post-bureaucratic ones.

THE IMPAIRED WORK GROUP

I would like briefly to consider the question of organizational cathexis in the context of the institutions of the Welfare State, a formation which, as has already been suggested, has a fundamentally contradictory nature within industrial capitalism. Claus Offe (1984) makes the vital point that Western capitalism can neither live with the Welfare State nor can it live without it. It is, at the same time, both Labour's proudest achievement and yet also integral to the legitimization and reproductive requirements of capital. The Welfare State is neither 'ours' nor 'theirs' but at the same time, in a way that satisfies neither, it belongs to both of us. In a twisted sort of way the Welfare State does stand for a way of responding to and providing for human need outside the market mechanism. To this extent it *can* be considered as the germ of a new society within the body of an old one.

For the time being at least, 'human value' remains an integral component of Welfare State institutions. Although the service ethic has become somewhat degraded, not least through the way in which it has furthered professional groups' own self-interest, it nevertheless remains a genuine motivational factor for the majority of individuals entering the public service area. The problem is that people are drawn in on the basis of a normative orientation to institutions in which such an orientation cannot be realized. In other words, such institutions contain the value-dimension missing from purely instrumental regimes, but contain it within a set of constraints which make the realization of such values for ever unobtainable. The sense of substantive purpose is therefore just sufficient to provide a sense of containment without resort to the wholesale simulation of the internal organizational world but, whilst organizational experience is in this sense 'real', it is also an experience of something profoundly impaired or damaged. Hence the institutional body takes on the form of an impaired body: clumsy, insensitive and thick-skinned.

Margot Waddell (1989), speaking of her experience of health care and social work institutions, draws out a crucial distinction between 'care and attention' on the one hand and 'servicing' on the other. Part of the reason why 'human service' has become a degraded term is that, from its inception, the Welfare State has been structured and resourced to a degree just sufficient to allow reasonable levels of 'public servicing' whilst precluding the possibility of real care and attention. Speaking of such institutions she remarks upon the sheer quantity of work to be done by the caring professions, a pressure which has the effect of 'effectively eliminating a space for thinking, for digesting experience, in the very area in which one would think it was most necessary' (p. 14). In such contexts action becomes a substitute for the pain of thought for, make no mistake, many state workers have profoundly painful jobs to do. As a colleague and I put it recently, such workers 'constitute an institutionalized buffer between the blandness and complacency of the public world and the intensity of private and privatized need and distress, whether this takes the form of abused children, battered wives, homeless families or neglected elderly people' (Hoggett and McGill, 1988, p. 31).

Working as a consultant within public sector settings one is constantly faced with the problem of repairing the damaged institutional body sufficiently to enable it to contain the painfulness of the reality of its internal and external environment. Only from such a position can public service workers retain what Kleinians would call the 'depressive position', that is, a commitment to the object in spite of its damaged state achieved by keeping inside onself and inside the group the image of a repaired object, and therefore the possibility of a better future. In my experience this means harnessing people's anger to the love that brought them to their work in the first instance. It is a love which often has no place in the life of the public institution. It is a love which, as Menzies (1959) found, is often regarded as 'unprofessional', something to be contained tightly within oneself, lest it upset the smooth running of the efficient human service factory. By such means anger must be harnessed in the struggle for the future, for the alternative lies in cynical withdrawal and destructive attack upon the very possibility of more human society. As such, I find myself no longer adopting the neutral psychoanalytic attitude with the organizations to which I act as consultant but more the position of a reflexive partisan.

There are signs that the Tavistock tradition of applying psychoanalytic principles to the study of group and organizational behaviour may be moving towards a more morally engaged position, and it is to this that I would now like to turn.

COLLUSION AND RESPONSIBILITY IN THE 'GROUP RELATIONS' TRADITION

We have already suggested that Bion's analysis of the Work Group is somewhat cursory to say the least. Within the tradition of group relations work which emerged around the Tavistock Institute in the ensuing decades one can detect the influence of Bion through various routes but particularly through the emergence of the idea of 'the primary task' – an assumed prerequisite for Work Group as opposed to Basic Assumption activity. This notion is still central to many who work within this tradition; for example, it provides the conceptual anchor for the Leicester Conferences, now run jointly by the Tavistock Institute for Group Relations and the Tavistock Clinic.

My sense is that Bion's original notion of the Work Group was a mythical construct, an empty term, a bit like his conception of alpha-function, and an invitation to subsequent generations to insert meaning into this under-developed container. The Tavistock tradition appropriated this concept through the medium of open-systems theory and in the process inevitably corrupted it. As a consequence, the concept of 'primary task' became not only a reified term but a term which both hid and deceived. Moreover, its usage has colluded with and reinforced those v‿ry tendencies towards shallowness in institutional life that the psychoanalytic perspective has otherwise endeavoured to appeal against.

Let us start, then, with a definition of 'primary task'. The definition comes from A. K. Rice: 'every enterprise, or part enterprise, has, however, at any given time a primary task – the task it must perform to survive' (1976, p. 26). Rice adds that, in order to survive, a group or institution may be considered as an open system which must exchange materials with its environment through an 'import–conversion–export' process. The task of organizational research and consultancy is to find an effective match between intra-organizational systems and environmental systems, in particular through the way in which the boundary between the two systems is managed (that is, the management of the 'relatedness' of institution to environment). Miller (1979, p. 218) lists two essential propositions which flow from this schema: first, 'a change in the relatedness of a system to its environment requires internal changes within the system: it must shift to a new steady state if it is to survive'; secondly, 'significant internal changes within a system cannot be sustained unless consistent changes occur in the relatedness of the system to its environment'.

These two propositions can be more easily understood in terms of reactivity and proactivity. The first proposition refers to the 'organizational work' necessary to respond effectively to a changing environment. The second proposition refers to the 'environmental work' necessary if changes initiated within the institution are to have a chance of survival, something which can be achieved only by overcoming the recalcitrance and hostility of the wider interorganizational environment.

The position adopted by the Miller/Rice tradition can be criticized from a number of angles. First of all it tends towards a crude functionalism in which organizations are constituted in reified fashion as phenomena having their own needs, goals and reproductive mechanisms. The very language of systems theory borrows from the modes of functioning (cybernetics and, more recently, ecology) of non-human systems where, as is particularly the case of biological and organic matter, the relationship between self-reproduction and survival (of the organism or species) appears self-evident. Yet, to use a crass but pertinent example, no one would ask stag beetles what right, that is, for what purpose, they have to survive as a species. But the predicament of the human species is precisely this, it is the only one for whom the question of the purpose of survival has any meaning. If survival for survival's sake becomes our rationale, then we may as well all become stag beetles: at least we would have a better chance of surviving nuclear war.

Thus to define 'primary task', as Rice does, in terms of that which the organization must perform in order to survive is to abandon the idea of substantive purpose in favour of that which is merely efficacious. Even if we were to reduce the concept of primary task to that of organizational goal or objective, the Tavistock tradition still stands guilty of gross naivety for the point is that, even in profit-making organizations, objectives are far from unproblematic. An accumulating mass of evidence points to the fact that even at their most senior levels private corporations are far from consensual masses pulling towards profit maximization; rather, they are political arenas in which different baronies and mafias fight for opposing interests or in pursuit of opposing visions of the 'way forward' (Bacharach and Lawler, 1980). Far from a 'primary task' being some kind of 'given', objectives are continually contested and, whilst some may come to dominate over others, impermanence of objective is the rule rather than the exception.

Moving from private companies to public institutions, the concept of primary task becomes still more problematic. Not only are public institutions (hospitals, schools, social services departments) made up of a series of loosely coupled domains (Weick, 1976), all of which press the requirements of their respective structural interest groups (Alford, 1975; Benson, 1982), but, more importantly, most of these institutions are themselves contained within the wider form of the Welfare State which, I have argued, has an essentially contradictory location within Western democracies. From this point of view the Welfare State represents a compromise, constantly subject to contestation and renegotiation, between the requirements of capital and labour. For its part, capital can neither live with the Welfare State (because its revenue needs precipitate a tendency towards fiscal crisis) nor live without it (though the New Right is trying its damnedest to dismantle as much public welfare as possible without courting electoral disaster).

So the Welfare State belongs to both classes but at the same time belongs properly to neither; it constrains inequality while at the same time reproducing it; it provides a medium for the democratization of the state whilst ensuring the 'statification' of democracy, and so on. The conflicting and multiple objectives which weigh so heavily upon many staff within public service institutions are therefore no more than the expression of the fundamentally divided purpose of the modern Welfare State; hence the relevance of the idea of the Impaired Work Group when acting as consultant to such institutions.

The Miller/Rice tradition represents a bizarre congealing of open-systems theory and psychoanalysis which, not surprisingly, has never been properly integrated. The psychoanalytic element has found its most powerful expression in the Group Relations Conferences, particularly the Leicester Conferences which have run without interruption since 1957. Within these events questions of human responsibility and value are absolutely central, the problem being that such conference events represent for many participants, staff and ordinary members a 'capsule' within which the meaning of 'full human relationship' can be apprehended in isolation from the dirty world outside.

However, I do get the feeling that this tradition is finally beginning to emerge from the cocoon of instrumental reason in which it had embedded itself through a realization that questions of value, when applied by consultants or change agents to public or private institutions, are always potentially explosive. In a recent critique of his own use of open-systems theory, Miller concludes with a revealing piece of self-reflection which is worth citing in full:

> I myself have written elsewhere that 'It is on [the member's] own authority to decide what to do with this understanding in his roles in other institutions, whether as manager or managed. However, I acknowledge that I personally hope that he will acquire greater potency to question and perhaps change his relationship with his personal environment.' (Miller, 1977, p. 44)
>
> But is this good enough? If learning can be sustained only through change, do I not have to risk taking *a moral stance* in relation to possible changes? (Miller, 1979, p. 232)

Let us remind ourselves of Primo Levi's dictum that, in the post-Auschwitz world, we can no longer afford the luxury of being 'unarmed'. If the application of psychoanalysis to the public sphere is to have the explosive impact that one guesses Bion would have hoped for, then questions of value cannot any longer be split off and dissociated from questions of technique. Such forms of institutionalized shallowness have been the subject of this chapter. It is to be hoped that Bion's successors within the Tavistock Group Relations tradition will join the side of those interrogating the problem rather than being a part of the problem that we face. They say that fear concentrates the mind wonderfully. Perhaps the threatened status of the Tavistock Institute and Clinic will finally alert sleeping minds to the armed detachments we now all face.

NOTES

1 As a result of this equation Etzioni's category of 'alienative organizations' is necessarily limited to prisons and the like in which physical constraint is used to bind participants to the institution. Etzioni fails to recognize the existence of other categories of constraint which, while non-physical in nature, are equally powerful in binding participants to regimes that are oppressive and brutal. Specifically, Marx's whole analysis of alienated labour is based upon the idea that a society had been created in which the great mass of individuals had no recourse but to work within the factory system if they wished to survive. Whilst the creation of the Welfare State to some degree weakened the sting of economic necessity, the recent revival of interest in 'workfare' schemes reconstructs the original 'no exit' situation facing landless households in Marx's time: if you don't work you get no money!

2 The British satirist Harry Enfield created the character 'Loadsamoney' as a way of representing the combination of wealth, vulgarity and inanity which has come to symbolize the 'wide boys' of London and the Home Counties and specifically the City of London. Despite the sheer awfulness of the character portrayed, 'Loadsamoney' quickly became a folk hero within the very subculture that he was designed to mock. A friend of mind noted recently that at a football match between Barnsley (a depressed mining community in the North of England) and Brighton the visiting supporters from the South waved £5 notes in the air to the chant of 'loadsamoney' as a way of goading the home team's followers.

7

In Love and Fear of the Group

As I have suggested before, a modern partisan movement can no longer afford to underestimate the recalcitrance of the material which it seeks to transform. One part of this task is to develop an adequate theory of subjectivity: one which recognizes the ultimate irreducibility of the individual to the social context and hence avoids the temptation to become another ideology of social engineering. Yet to understand ourselves as human beings who are also natural beings, as the intersection of nature and culture, is no easy task.

A vital part of this understanding is the recognition that the 'naturalness' of humanity resides in its corporeality. Despite 'the wonders of civilization' and the extension of human powers it has given rise to, despite the fact that many of us live in a world of flickering images and manufactured domesticity, we remain corporeal beings. We are born into a period of extended helplessness; we live and then we die. These are the simple facts of life and death which we all know about. Yet to understand their personal meaning, that is, their meaning not as objective, external fact but as personal destiny, seems for ever beyond our grasp. Self-consciousness is indeed both our opportunity and our curse and, whilst we might become engaged through life in all kinds of worthy preoccupations, in silent moments we cannot fail to notice the wearing of our bodies or the prompting of our dreams.

The great strength of psychoanalysis has resided in its insistent search for the body in the mind, for the corporeal in the cultural. It has constantly endeavoured to bring us back down to earth, to reveal the 'primitive' foundation of all 'higher' forms: the gnawing hunger of doubt, the digestibility of thought, the body of the group (the *esprit de corps*), the genitality of weapons and the anality of money. At times, yes, its zealousness had led it towards self-parody in which its earnest deliberations, to the outsider, resemble end-of-the-pier smuttiness. I would be the first to admit that my own reading of some of Freud's or Klein's case studies has been the occasion for sudden bouts of great hilarity. Psychoanalysis has not been short on myth. How else could it be when so much of it had turned its back on external reality? When Freud turned his back on seduction theory to seek the origin of psychic trauma solely in terms of internal phantasy rather than real abuse he really did let the father get away with murder. And yet he himself was never fully convinced, as his efforts to reconstruct a theory of actual trauma in the early 1920s disclose.[1]

To my mind the difficulty psychoanalytic theory has had in providing a conceptual space which can contain internal and external realities is properly resolved only by certain post-Freudian developments. And the key seems to have been the realization that the body is fundamentally an intersubjective body, our corporeality a social corporeality. Until this point psychoanalysis remained trapped within a 'psychological monadism' (Bercherie, 1986), where the individual was posited in terms of a closed system of conflictual impulses and their attendant phantasies. External reality existed only as something shadowy and insubstantial; the real dramas went on elsewhere, that is, within the sealed internal world of the infant or neurotic adult.

To my mind the key shift towards a properly social psychoanalysis occurred through the work of Winnicott and Bion. Each writer in his own way returns to Freud's remarks in *The Ego and the Id* (1923) that the ego is at first a bodily ego, but they extend this notion through an insistence that the infant's first sense of itself as a corporeal being occurs by virtue of its being in relation to another. The starting point is not 'the one' but 'the relationship'. The infant does not exist except in so far as it figures in a relationship with another who cares. And at first this relationship is above all a physical relationship; a physical crucible within which sensation and experience are given some place or space in which to find expression. The dominant image is of the physical space of the mother's embrace, that is, the space derived from being held and cuddled close to the parent's body. Here, then, is the first place, the first experience of form and shape; a contained space which is neither internal and subjective nor external, for at this stage such terms have no meaning. Again, to return to Freud's (1923) notion of consciousness as 'contact boundary'; the first contact boundary is this relationship of bodies, of physical skin surfaces, to be found in the nurturing embrace. Speaking of the ego, Freud remarks that it is 'not merely a surface entity, but is itself the projection of a surface' (p. 16).

What we need to think of, then, is the parental embrace as the original prototype of a space which, with development, becomes more properly a psychical space, the inner space of subjectivity. Winnicott uses the term 'psyche-soma' (1949) to refer to this original prototype which is neither mind nor body but that physical and emotional relationship in which sensation and experience first find containment. But it is not just the infant who brings emotionality into this enclosed space; the parent does so, too. Again an elusive term, but one which brings us closer to an understanding of what the parent brings, is Bion's notion of the other's 'reverie'. The parental embrace is not just a physical embrace for, when the parents hold the infant they hold a part of themselves. It must be so. Failure here dooms the infant to a life of pure externality: without parental cathexis that first embrace is without meaning, and if the infant has no meaning it remains an 'it'. The task of development is to pass from experience to subjective experience, from a limitless and boundaryless world which bombards the infant with environmental and bodily stimuli to the bounded subjectivity in which events have some locus and value. In Freud's immortal words: 'Where "it" was there "I" shall be.'

When we say that at first the infant's world is an undifferentiated world, it is worth stopping to consider what this means in terms of the infant's actual experience. We get close to some kind of understanding by pursuing the idea that undifferentiatedness means no inside or outside, no me or not-me. We see an infant on a blanket in a lit room, with a soiled nappy; it may be hungry and we are talking. But the infant may just as easily experience a light which seems to be the source of a gnawing pain and a noise which it lies upon providing damp support. Without boundaries with which to locate and place experience, life must be chaotic – a booming, budding confusion, as William James put it.

For Bion and Winnicott, when the parent picks up and cuddles the infant this embrace provides the first potential space in which the unintegrated fragments of experience can be ordered and given some meaning. This space is at first a primarily physical space, constructed by the relationship between two bodies. By insisting that the ego is at first a bodily ego, Freud suggests that the first glimmerings of a sense of self emerge from a body (self) consciousness. But we would now add that in the beginning the body is an intersubjective body: there is not the one but two, united through the embrace. The problem to resolve is not, then, 'how is the social bond created?'; if development is to occur at all the bond must be there in the beginning.

Before the development of a psychoanalysis grounded in intersubjectivity, the discipline was inevitably reductionist. Nowhere was this more manifest than in psychoanalytic attempts to grasp the nature of group phenomena. One can trace a long line, from Freud's original *Group Psychology and the Analysis of the Ego* (1921) to the contemporary writing of Chasseguet-Smirgel (1985a,b) which comes to grips with the psychology of the group only by essentially reducing it to an intrapsychic phenomenon.

What is at issue is not the nature of the social bond but the nature of its disruption and perversion in social life. Let us remind ourselves again of Bion's opening remarks in his essay, 'Group dynamics':

> The adult must establish contact with the emotional life of the group in which he lives; this task would appear to be as formidable to the adult as the relationship with the breast appears to be to the infant. (1961, pp. 141–2)

First, let us note that the statement implies that, whilst we all live in groups, this does not mean that we are in emotional contact with them. Secondly, a variety of forms of emotional contact is undoubtedly possible. One may, for example, be adhesively identified with a group, clinging to its surface, that is, to its fantasy of itself. On the other hand, one may be a part of the body of the group rather than adhering to its outer skin; one may, for instance, be the 'eyes and ears' of the group or the shoulder upon which the group is carried. Alternatively, one may be a part of a group which does not now have a proper 'body of members', a dismembered group, a collection of subgroup particles, the detritus left from a group which fell apart. Note, we are positing an original language of the group, that is, the group as the em-body-ment of intersubjectivity. As Anzieu notes (1984, p. 124), this language goes deep into our history; for example, according to St Paul, we are 'the body of Christ and individually members of it'. Note also how this original language, this language of our original nature, is being displaced by the language of the machine, of the system.

PSYCHOANALYSIS AND THE FEAR
OF THE GROUP

Lacking a proper understanding of the intersubjective grounding of inte-
riority, of selfhood, classical psychoanalysis endeavours to approach the
group using a different language, the language of the symbolic family form,
the family of Oedipus. Now it could be argued, as indeed Bion at one time
alluded in passing (1961 p. 187), that the 'family group' is the original group
from which all other social forms can be read. The problem is that we know
in reality that there is no single family form but many family forms; indeed,
'family' itself may well be an element of a class rather than a super-ordinate
category in its own right. Within classical psychoanalysis the family does
not have the status of 'the real' but of a symbolic universality which derives
its status from the role it is called upon to enact – as foil to the internal play
of the individual's phantasy life. To restate the point, the abandonment of
the theory of actual trauma for a theory of traumatic phantasy was equivalent to an abandonment of the real but contingent family for the symbolic
universal family. With this shift, real mothers and real fathers become
eclipsed by symbolic mothers and symbolic fathers. According to Freud,
the latter constitute the players necessary for enacting life's formative drama
– drama of the oedipal complex – after which all other dramas are mere
repetitions and out of which our structured subjectivity first emerges.

From this classical position all social forms become re-enactments. The
account differs only over whether group life is a form of working through
of our relationship with our oedipal father or with our pre-oedipal mother.
A statement of Chasseguet-Smirgel summarizes the difference between her
own account and that of Freud in a precise manner:

> the leader is not the father's substitute; on the contrary he is the man
> who implicitly promises the coming of a world without any father and
> a correlative union with the almighty mother. (1985a, p. 61)

I see little point in dwelling upon which account gets close to the truth; the
accounts differ only in emphasis, they are each locked in the mythologized
problematic of the universal family.

Reading *Group Psychology and the Analysis of the Ego* (1921) one cannot
but be struck by Freud's preoccupation with the army general as the
archetype of all leadership: stern, watchful and strong. On the other hand,
reading Chasseguet-Smirgel it becomes clear that the topic for dissection is

not the group leader but the group illusion, that is, its ideological illusion. So, whereas Freud seeks the nature of the social bond in a collective identification with a harsh super-ego father figure, Chasseguet-Smirgel traces it to an identification with a seductive and archaic maternal ego-ideal figure. Although the fit is not precise, one is reminded here of the distinction Bion (1961) draws between the dependency group leader and the 'messianic idea' which fulfils the leadership function in the pairing group.

I do not want to diminish the value of either of these two approaches. They both throw light upon important group phenomena which undoubtedly exist. What I wish to draw attention to is the way in which each account essentially posits the group as a dangerous phenomenon from which psychoanalysis offers a form of consolation through its conception of a mature individualism.[2]

Whilst Freud (1921) felt that Le Bon had been too hard on the group, there is little in his own analysis to suggest that he had a more generous attitude. For Freud, the group is nearly always construed simply as an invitation to regression. Groups bring out the worst in us. What solace there is (and there is precious little in Freud's view of life) must be wrung by settling accounts with oneself. To turn outwards through action on and within the social world is almost inevitably an attempt to deny, through action, painful inner reality: politics is the last refuge of the scoundrel. By such a route, for much of this century, psychoanalysis has developed its own distinctive ideology: an ideology of grim and quietistic individualism into which we can withdraw from a real world which, when at last it is admitted as existing, is seen as 'out of control' and terrifying. The group as a positive, creative and constructive force is virtually absent from these accounts and, hence, if our social nature is conceded to it is conceded in a grumbling fashion, almost as a curse rather than as our fortune.

Let us explore this some more. For one thing this negative view of social nature leads Freud and Chasseguet-Smirgel to disparage the very notion of collective sentiment. Where others might see the existence of 'solidarity' and 'collective identity' these writers see only social defences against sibling rivalry. From this point of view the very idea of fraternity is a lie. The position is spelt out perfectly by Freud in a phrase that Chasseguet-Smirgel repeats triumphantly fifty years later: 'if one cannot be the favourite oneself, at all events nobody else shall be the favourite' (1985a, p. 52). In saying this Freud had just ruled out the possibility of there being a primary social instinct. According to Freud, the child alone is not comforted by the sight of any other; each child would like to be 'the only one' but 'in consequence of the impossibility of his maintaining his hostile attitude without damaging himself, he is forced into identifying himself with other children' (1923, p. 27). This original defence against envy is for Freud the prototype of all forms of 'identification among equals' within later group life.

Viewed from this position, one should not be surprised therefore to discover that beneath the surface bonhomie of comradeship lurks a sup- pressed hatred and destructiveness. This is fuelled further by the ambi- valence of the group member *vis-à-vis* the father-leader, admiration for whom conceals an original phantasy of patricide. Within Chasseguet-Smir- gel's schema the father-leader is chased away from the group for, whilst strong, as super-ego representative, he is also the locus of constraint. The group's ideology binds its members through identification with a common ego-ideal; in this messianic position the group lacks conscience and with the removal of this locus of instinctual prohibition it becomes capable of all kinds of reprehensible acts in the name of its ideal.

Clearly, from either account, the group must do something with its suppressed hatred, and it is at this point that another actor is summoned to make an appearance: 'the other', the out-group. In a historical frame of mind Freud notes: 'If another group tie takes the place of the religious one – and the socialistic tie seems to be succeeding in doing so – then there will be the same intolerance towards outsiders as in the age of the Wars of Religion' (1921, pp. 30–1). Chasseguet-Smirgel notes, even more stridently: 'It is indeed impossible for a group based upon an ideology not to be proselytizing and not to seek to destroy not only its enemies, but also those who remain outside it' (1985b, p. 87). Significantly she adds that this is equivalent to the attitude 'that those who are not with us are against us'. As Meltzer (1978) had noted on an earlier occasion this kind of attitude is Old Testament stuff.

So the failure of much of psychoanalysis to situate itself within the discourse of intersubjectivity leads it to develop a one-sided, negative critique of the group and its attendant forms of sociability, identity and solidarity. It is not too difficult to detect within this an explicitly reactionary ideological position. In particular we should note that much of the target of this critique is the group when considered as social movement, that is, as a crowd, a religious or political force. Such accounts conspicuously fail to offer a corresponding critique of the group considered in its other major social form, as a stable, inert, imprisoning institution.

In this light an article by Reicher and Potter (1985) is very illuminating. They are concerned to examine some of the unconscious assumptions within early group psychology, particularly in the work of Le Bon and McDougall. Given the size of Freud's own debt to Le Bon, discernible from reading the opening sections of Freud's *Group Psychology* (1921), their analysis is therefore relevant to an understanding of psychoanalytic group psychology. It is interesting to note, then, that from the outset Reicher and Potter are at pains to criticize the early group psychologists for reducing crowd behaviour to 'intra-individual events thereby ignoring the social conflict and social oppression which led crowd members to take action'. Reicher and Potter suggest that for these early writers 'the crowd became the active symbol of social breakdown', and their science can be read as an expression of an 'acute crisis of confidence' undergone by bourgeois culture of late nineteenth-century Europe. In other words, the motive for explanation in early group psychology came from the desire to contain social movements; movements which could only seem alien, foreign and outside the experience of a social élite which, despite its enlightenment, could not comprehend them. As 'outsiders' such early group psychologists were quite unable to identify the reasons for crowd members' behaviour and hence depicted it as 'unreasonable', in the double sense of being 'without reason' and 'pathological'. The crowd was collective pathology; crowd behaviour was reduced to the fusing of intra-individual predispositions; 'the other' was absent except as an almost accidental victim of this collective frenzy, as something which happens to be in the wrong place at the wrong time and gets consumed by the herd-crowd as it crashes by.

Of course, what is missing from the accounts of the early group psychologists, and from the later accounts of Freud and Chasseguet-Smirgel, is an understanding that social movements typically move against something: the movement opposes its power to another power, a power which, if not constitutive of that movement at the outset, is at least inextricably tied up with the life and death of that movement. When miners, black youth or students riot, there will be irrational phantasies, displaced aggression and messianic longings, but there will also be a real other, be it the Anglo-American Mining Company, the Metropolitan Police Force or the university authorities. By pathologizing all social movements, the work of making psychoanalysis really applicable to the public sphere becomes all the harder. Social movements do lie to themselves, do seek solace in consoling myth rather than hard truth, do seek easy targets for difficult feelings, do fracture into warring and mutually uncomprehending bands. To be effective, movements need to know when and why this is happening, for only in such ways can they be properly reflexive and critical. With the possible exception of Touraine's (1981) work with the French anti-nuclear movement, psychoanalysis has not been received by social movements in this way; rather, it is regarded as a bourgeois and reactionary science which seeks to destroy or keep the same rather than enabling change. Maybe this is as Freud would have wanted it. How appropriate, therefore, that psychoanalysis, when considered as a social movement in its own right, should have displayed all the pathologies listed above and more. Moreover, it has been quite unable to be reflexive about much of the mess which passes for its own history!

CREATIVE UNREASON

This fear of the group, which is in part, no doubt, an expression of pure ideology (a mask for fear and contempt of the 'dangerous classes') but is also a response to the real experience of mass movements (fascistic, fundamentalist) in the twentieth century, leaves us with no choice but to reconstitute 'the group' as a formative, creative, benign phenomenon. We must bring the group-baby back in from the mob-bathwater. The simple issue is this: if groups are so regressive, so deluded, so paranoid, so blind and so dangerous, how come they have been responsible for nearly all the major advances in science, in politics, in industry and even in culture? Could Freud have produced, as he did, without his group, his network and Klein? Indeed, the only major figure within psychoanalysis who appears to have produced, as it were in isolation, is Fairbairn, beavering away in the Scottish lowlands far away from the circles gathered in and around London NW3.

It is towards more contemporary developments, which provide psychoanalysis with a properly relational foundation, that we must look for an adequate theorization of the group. In my examination of the institutionalization of shallowness I have already noted how Bion, through his notion of the Work Group, provides the conceptual space within which a psychodynamic understanding of non-pathological groups can be developed. We have also noted how Bion himself provided little more than this. His theorization of the Work Group remained almost entirely unelaborated as his attention was drawn to its psychopathological shadow, that is, to the

Basic Assumption Groups. I also suggested that Weber's concept of substantive rationality provides the only adequate basis for an understanding of group or institutional purpose; a form of purpose in which moral, aesthetic and technical considerations remain properly integrated. According to Bion, the existence of an agreed purpose is an essential condition for the establishment of Work Group activity.

With these considerations in mind I feel it is now possible to begin an exploration of the phenomenon of group life which, whilst being non-rationalistic, is also non-reductionist. Why is this necessary? Why bother with a psychoanalytic perspective, given that for much of this century such perspectives have been employed largely to disparage the political project rather than sustain it?

The answer is simple and obvious. It should hardly need stating; that such an effort is necessary should give us pause for thought. The essential problem is that all forms of socialist thought, with the possible exception of some anarchist and libertarian currents, have been excessively rationalistic. They have placed their faith in analysis, in programme, in having 'the correct ideas' and have lost sight of the role of faith, imagination, desire and the unconscious as sources both of mobilization and passion and of passivity and self-subjugation. In this sense we might admit that socialism has borrowed too much from instrumental rationality, that one-sided calculus of human behaviour which was its own mortal enemy. And perhaps, given the dominance of men within such socialist traditions, we should not be too surprised that it has adopted this narrowly patriarchal method as its own. A politics of change which is not also a politics of emotion, passion, unreason and the dream is a strange and cold politics indeed. The tragedy is that those, like Marcuse (1964), who looked to psychoanalysis for the missing 'side' of politics drew upon the early pre-relational psychoanalytic tradition for guidance and in doing so moved from a dialectical model to a conflict model which pitted the individual against a totally administered society. Psychoanalytic Marxism could not, from this position, develop a means of understanding the contradictoriness of human nature. Classical psychoanalysis tends to apprehend social nature as something essentially external to, rather than intrinsic to, human nature. Rather than seeing the individual as a lived contradiction between nature and humanity, psychoanalysis has tended to see only conflict between individual and society. In so doing it fails to grasp both the social nature of the individual and the physical (corporeal) basis of all social forms.

We can begin to assemble a more two-sided picture of the group by considering the demonstrable confusion psychoanalysis has generated concerning illusion and delusion. For it is as if, following Freud, psychoanalysis (despite its own better knowledge) can bring itself to think of the role of illusion in society only in its negative sense, as deception. Winnicott (1974)[3] is the only exception here; it is as if he were left to spell out what the others could not bring themselves to say: that without illusion there is no culture, no playing, no spontaneity. For Winnicott, subjectivity finds expression not primarily through some kind of solitary 'I', a pure unity created only by reflecting upon itself, but through the space in between 'inner' and 'outer', between 'the self' and 'the given'. This transitional space is neither purely internal nor external but the space where they conjoin. Where a 'dualistic' epistemology sees a boundary marking off the frontiers of two separate realities, Winnicott sees an area, an area where nothing is simply 'given' or simply 'hallucinated'. In this sense illusion is the realm of 'the not yet'; it is the space of the possible. The *Shorter Oxford English Dictionary* speaks of delude as 'to cause what is false to be accepted as true'. Were, then, the North Vietnamese deluded in thinking that they, a peasant army, could defeat the might of French and American Imperialism? Were the Afghans similarly deluded, and the Jewish partisans, and the tiny Bolshevik party in 1917? The problem with hindsight of course is that it encourages smug prognostications about unreason. Those, therefore, who would dissect mass movements in order to disclose a phenomenon in the grip of unreason should ponder that the balance of forces is never 'a given' but always a fluid and changeable quantity. Despite their leaders' tactics, how close the British miners came to defeating the Thatcher Government in the late summer of 1985![4]

If it is true that children never entirely give up their illusions of omnipotence (nor should they) so it is also true that the group should beware of those 'friends' who warn it against having illusions of grandeur. The issue is not whether the group should resort to myth-making or not; it is in the very nature of the group to have its myth, as Freud well knew. The issue is whether the group is condemned by its myths, in their thrall, as it were, or whether it can use its own mythology in the process of creation. Psychodynamically speaking 'the myth' can be regarded as an object; the issue is whether the group can emerge from the position of object-relating to object-usage. Are its myths to be used as a material of production, as an aspect of the group's productive forces? In other words, can they be used for work or only for consolation?

An essential characteristic of illusion as used by Winnicott (1974), Milner (1955) and Ogden (1986) is its 'as if' quality. This is expressed most clearly in the analytic relationship itself, where the creative use of the transference has precisely this quality about it. As Ogden notes, the mature transference (as opposed to delusional transference) 'involves the capacity to generate an illusion that is experienced simultaneously as real and not real' (1986, p. 239). This is, of course, precisely the same kind of illusion generated by a writer through a work of fiction or by a dramatist in staging a play. The question, 'Is this real or fantasy?', is never put; for illusion to succeed the spell must not be broken. I was once a member or a very small but, I feel, highly creative political group. We produced an occasional journal called *Intervention* and were known publicly as the Intervention Collective. Privately we called ourselves 'the Famous Five', a label which has warm but slightly ridiculous connotations for anybody who was brought up as a child within mid-twentieth-century British culture.[5] We wanted to change the world, or at least a small part of it, and we were serious about this. Omniscience in itself is no bad thing. How much of what we call civilization could have been created without such illusions of grandeur? But this was an omniscience which knew about itself, it was the creative use of un-reason. But *delusions* of grandeur are something else, lacking any element of humour or reflexivity they can, too literally, become deadly serious.

SHARED PLAYING

Milner (1955, p. 98), speaking of the social psychological space in which creativity occurs, speaks of the need for 'a medium' between internal and external realities. This medium is the pliable stuff of Winnicott's 'potential space', that third reality which is neither entirely internally generated nor externally unalterable; 'the interplay between there being nothing but me and there being objects and phenomena outside omnipotent control' (Winnicott, 1974, p. 118). Clearly clay exemplifies this medium, hence no doubt the centrality of this substance in the psychodynamic work with children, a tradition which began with Melanie Klein. But all of science, culture and politics works through a medium of one form or another, the common characteristic being 'this pliable stuff that can be made to take the shape of one's phantasies' (Milner, 1955, p. 99).

My feeling is that the notion of the 'pliable medium' provides the link between the creativity of the child or artist at play and the creativity of the individual or group intervening in social systems, whether such systems refer to the micro-level of the institution or small community or the grander level of the culture and politics of whole societies.

Consider, for example, the action space of individuals within institutional settings. I am reminded here of the work of Rosemary Stewart (1982) with managers in public and private-sector organizations. Stewart's research was illuminating for the way in which it indicated that the space an individual perceived for making changes within organizational settings was constituted by the interpenetration of subjective and objective factors. She discovered, for example, that managers operating in identical settings would nevertheless perceive that they had widely different space for taking action. This 'room for manoeuvre' was partly determined by the actual demands and constraints impinging upon managers but also, and crucially, by their differing perceptions of these demands and constraints. Stewart attempted to 'get inside', that is, provide a phenomenology of this action space by encouraging managers to construe demands through the simple

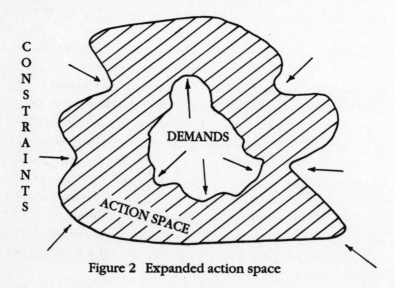

Figure 2 Expanded action space

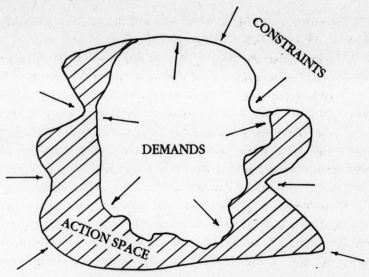

Figure 3 Constricted action space

phrase, 'I have to . . . or else' and constraints through the simple phrase, 'I can't . . . because'. Diagrammatically we can therefore contrast the action space of two individuals in identical institutional settings as shown in Figures 2 and 3.

Clearly her model is over-simplified in a number of ways, not the least because it doesn't enable us to consider how the perceived action space may be expanded once the effect of collective action for change is brought into the picture. Nevertheless, it does provide us with a 'way in' to thinking about how Winnicott's notion of potential space can be applied to the whole issue of human agency in social systems. I am suggesting that social relations themselves, as they operate in family, work or other institutions, constitute the 'pliable medium' of potential space: that space in between (the individual or group) desire and imagination on the one hand and, on the other, inertial externality, 'the repudiated world, the not-me, that which the individual has decided to recognize (with whatever difficulty and even pain) as truly external, which is outside magical control' (Winnicott, 1974, p. 47).

Bringing the ideas of Stewart and Winnicott together we can begin to visualize an intermediate reality which different writers have glimpsed in

different ways in terms of action space, potential space, room for manoeuvre, 'elbow room' (Meltzer *et al.*, 1986, p. 39). Human agency assumes
the existence of this potential space. It is the space between imagination
and its realization, between the conceived and the real(ized) object of
production, between psychical and physical realities. Without a playful and
interrogative attitude, the external world remains frozen and fixed, demanding our compliance. Only by virtue of such a playful attitude does it
become unfrozen and pliable. In the context of agency within social
systems, playfulness and reality-testing become inseparable. Creative
groups become energized through a series of interrogations of their social
context; interrogations which typically find expression through phrases
such as, 'What's to stop us from doing x?' In other words, it is only by testing
the limits of a situation that one can discover its actual, as opposed to its
assumed, boundaries. This is not a passive process of contemplation but
an active process of experimentation, of pushing at the limits. According to
Winnicott, 'In health the fetal impulses bring about a discovery of the
environment, this latter being the opposition that is met through movement,
and sensed during movement' (1950, p. 216). We speak of 'diving in',
'letting go', 'taking the plunge', and I think these phrases accurately express
the fluid and pliable nature of the social medium one immerses oneself in
when assuming agency in social systems. It is a fluidity derived in part from
the process of deconstructing internal and external realities, in part from
the absolute unpredictability of human environments, within which even
the best-laid plans may come to naught. We must be careful, however, not
to confuse 'pliability' with 'malleability'. The medium, though pliable, is not
infinitely so. In testing the limits of a situation, actual boundaries will be
discovered: boundaries which do not 'give' and opposition which is solid
and inertial in its quality. A playful, interrogative attitude is therefore a
necessary part of discovering the real configuration or grain of the social
material upon which one is working.

The phrase, 'working with the grain', reveals to us in a simple form the
point that Marx always insisted upon: for objectification[6] to occur the
labourer must recognize and respect the regularities of the material upon
which she works. But if this is the good sense within the phrase there is
also a bad sense, for it suggests that the material of production necessarily
assumes the nature of inert matter. But when we speak of non-material
production, the pliable medium consists of social relations into which we

seek to intervene and here we are always dealing with a dynamic equilibrium, a balance of conflicting or contradictory forces.

Kurt Lewin's force field analysis (1948) provides us with a model for thinking of 'the grain' within social systems. In any social or institutional setting, Lewin argues, 'the given' is always the outcome of a balance of forces both pushing for change and resisting change. In this sense reality is always contested, always in the nature of a compromise. Similarly, the partisan is always primarily concerned with the balance of forces: between forces and relations of production; between and within classes and institutions; between and within groups and even within oneself and between self and others. Above all, the partisan is concerned with the nature of their collision, the temporary solutions and compromises generated, the alliances and accommodations made between different forces, and, on the basis of this understanding, engages practically in strengthening some and undermining others.

How, then, is it that such a dynamic reality often seems so inert? There is a parallel here with what happens to systems of thought, whether these be collective systems like psychoanalysis or the individual's own thoughts about self, life and relationships. In Bion's terms, as soon as a new thought-system for containing experience becomes developed it tends to harden and atrophy: this is Bion's metaphor of the explosive force and the containing framework. Within social systems, resolutions to conflicts between groups, once constructed, tend to lose their dynamic quality as temporary compromises and become crystalline structures, things-in-themselves, reifications, means-become-ends. One thinks then of a social process which is sclerotic, a process of petrification, calcification or vitrification. One is reminded also of Freud's (1920) notion of tropism, of the tendency for all organic systems to return towards the state of the inorganic.

In part, the inertness of social reality is clearly a result of our own inability to sustain a creative and interrogative attitude towards it, which in itself is no more than an indication of the impossibility of sustaining our subjectivity *ad infinitum.* The point is simply this: freedom is exhausting; we get tired and must allow ourselves to relapse into unfreedom if we are to get by. This state of mind, which I have referred to as 'it-ness', is an expression of the conservative and restraining hand of nature within human nature. But we should distinguish between this necessarily uncreative aspect of our human nature and that which is the product of our fear, a fear of disturbing our own internal establishment, the establishment which is internal to the group of which we are a part and the establishment which becomes revealed when our own individual or collective creativity exposes the real, as opposed to imagined, forces which oppose our endeavours to bring about change within the social context. Fear of freedom is always a product of a terror which has both an internal and external locus.

INTERNAL AND EXTERNAL HEGEMONY

Whether we speak of the life of the mind, the life of the group or the life of society, we are always confronted by a ruling order whose hegemony tends to convert a dynamic equilibrium into an inertial set of 'givens'. It is an order which invites our consent to its domination. It is a governing order which has the conceit to speak of 'its subjects' when in reality its hegemony relies upon their self-subjugation. To use a phrase of Anderson (1976), within the state of hegemony, consent is dominant whilst coercion is determinant. Without coercion, without terror being present in the background, the establishment cannot engineer consent.

How might we picture terror? Think of the father, the threatening stranger, the torturer as its personifications. But what of terror unpersonified? Think of 'the wrath of God', 'the peoples' justice', 'the state's duty to preserve freedom'.

How is terror exercised? Essentially by not being explicit about the action intended. It keeps us in suspense, nurtures our uncertainty, persecutes us with doubt. Unlike fear, which is always of something known, terror is unknowable; thus it encourages our imagination to run riot.

> A patient who was imprisoned after 'disappearing' for a while recalled the intervals of time between each torture as moments of the greatest mental suffering, due to the absence of limits on his psychic pain. He was invaded by a state of panic, in which something totally unimaginable and incomprehensible, something terrible was going to happen, but without his knowing when or how. This state was experienced as one of insane uncertainty; during the torture, in contrast, he could limit the panic by dedicating himself to a defence against physical and mental pain. (Puget, 1988, p. 113)

Terror always keeps something in hand, never quite revealing all its cards; it cultivates an atmosphere by never delivering what it promises; it never 'puts an end' to things. The threat is always there, always worse than the actual punishment. A father or teacher who knows how to instil terror may never actually need to raise a hand. Terror summons the inconceivable; it makes present the unrepresentable in a raw but unspecific way. As Puget (1988, p. 112) suggests, this is akin to a state of threat, a cold dread which induces an internal regime of catastrophe and, whilst many may face a common terror, we each experience it in our aloneness.

This catastrophe was always present, hidden and buried in our person-alities. It is our Achilles' heel, one we all share by virtue of the contradiction at the heart of our being both of nature and yet beyond nature. It is this existential contradiction which is the locus of that most basic anxiety, catastrophic anxiety, that Klein and Bion knew so well. It is the anxiety of disintegration, of psychosis, portrayed variously by analysts as falling, annihilation, the dead end, the nameless dread. It is a falling through that space between our nature and our humanity where lost souls wander who have no place in either the natural or human universe. Jones (1927) spoke of it in terms of aphanisis, the prototype of all subsequent experiences of terror, including castrtion anxiety. it is the experience of a failed social medium, a medium which can no longer support our humanity, a kind of drowning. It is the thin ice or rent at the heart of our being, a fault which is always present, indwelling. Even that earliest phase of undifferentiated illusionment of which Winnicott speaks is never free from its contamina-tion. That moment at which the infant is catapulted from the amniotic sea into the waiting social medium must always leave its mark. Eden was never perfect; it was always haunted' by imminent catastrophe. Imminence – 'indwelling', 'actually present or abiding in' – a potential state of original terror from which we are for ever in flight. It is this that the establishment, internal and external, threatens us with by offering to remove its protection. It is in this way that it induces our submission and respect, beckons us to lead the life of the lie and reject the truth of our own experience. Life and death in the mind are always as much in the balance as life and death of culture and politics. Each lie is a deadening of experience, a process by which the vital stuff of life becomes cast into facticity. And this is the route by which hegemonic processes petrify and vitrify reality; it is the production of surplus objectivity.

Summarizing what has been said so far we can note how the creative impulse always faces two kinds of boundary, two kinds of opposition. The first is revealed through the playful and interrogative process of reality-testing, a process both constituted by and constitutive of the potential space within which culture is developed. One thinks of the kind of delight a young child feels in pushing over constructions; the more impressive they look, the greater the delight in knocking them down. It is the enjoyment of overcoming obstacles, sensing the 'give' within the 'given', opening up new possibilities. We interrogate our surroundings – the team within which we work, the community or cultural group to which we belong – through such cheekiness.

In this way we create a space for change, some room for manoeuvre, though, following Winnicott, we should not ask whether this space was created or whether it was already there. But the space is never unlimited. At a certain point we will have 'gone too far'; the disturbance which has been created has somehow become intolerable. We no longer face an opposition which is pliable, with a capacity for give and take, but something more rigid and menacing. The human environment, whether inside or outside us, has lost its capacity to preserve the depressive position from which our unprecedented actions could be apprehended as something novel and exciting; instead it has adopted a pre-depressive attitude from which such actions are seen as a threat.

It is at this point that creativity must lose its element of cheekiness. One is still at play, but now the game has two sides, and its consequences can be serious. Moreover, the creative impulse may well be up against several opponents working in partnership, as it were: the conservative elements in oneself, one's group and in the 'outside world'. Paradoxically then, the forces of change contain forces of resistance within themselves.

Consider the creative group in this light or, following Bion, what might be called the 'Revolutionary Work Group'. The body of the group, its corpus, is constituted through its collective desire and imagination; qualities which bind the group spontaneously, without recourse to simulation and without any need for formal discipline. Bion's notion of co-operation, though not misleading, hardly does justice to the electric-like nature of such a group. Rather, we might think of it at first as a 'free association', 'an association in which the free development of each is the condition of the free development of all'. But this is a freedom which must be protected for, in the very process of its creation, group members can envisage the possibility of betrayal.

A few years ago, part of my working life was consumed by just such a group. At that moment the group had just five members. We had worked together for years without ever really working together, if you see what I mean. Being grandiose for a moment, I should add that we were all very competent intellectuals and organizational consultants. We shared a common set of social priorities and had a vision of creating a new university centre focusing on the interpenetration of social values and institutional processes. I'm sorry if this sounds dull; to us it was very exciting! We had been meeting furtively for several months (we called ourselves the Furtive Five). This felt like a free association, the kind of group to which Polan (1984, p.188) refers, which can 'transact its business and pursue its goal with a speed, efficiency, willingness and comradeship that makes formal structures and procedures practically redundant'. Polan adds, 'Such a collective draws on an almost electric field of common assumptions and shared norms.' But almost from the outset we were each aware of the possibility of betrayal. This was not about defection, of joining 'the other side', for at that moment there were no sides to be drawn; rather, it was a fear of one's fellows not giving of themselves. The creative group demands one thing: the generosity of its members. It demands a collective giving, because it is this 'collective giving'. What is feared, then, is not defection, but the failure to give generously; for the group this is the one form of dissent which is difficult to tolerate.

This possibility, that one's comrades may differ in their commitment, arouses both psychotic and depressive anxieties; both the phantasy of the disintegration of the body of the group and the phantasy of its disfigurement. Without the capacity to contain such anxieties the group will inevitably rigidify, as Polan (1984, p. 189) notes: 'The moment of the apocalypse is thus followed by the pledge.' It is through this first resort to terror that the group creates a place for its own establishment. Following Sartre, Polan is clearly pessimistic about the group ever being able to contain such anxieties; the resort to terror becomes inevitable. As I will argue later, such pessimism is a consequence of the one-sided perspective that Sartre proposes; a perspective from which the group is pictured only as something in opposition to another power, not as something which can also be constituted by a positive vision, by a desire to create. The Sartrian group is locked in a life-or-death struggle with an external power from the very outset. In such situations the fear is not just one of lack of commitment but is one of betrayal, of group members going over to the other side.

The issue is not whether psychotic and depressive anxieties are a feature of the creative group; the issue is whether they are of such an intensity that no containment is possible. Either way, the containment of such anxiety will always be a matter of degree, and the construction of some kind of group establishment is therefore inevitable. The task is to create a culture or 'way of being' in the group which enhances its capacity to contain the potentially unbearable feelings of mistrust, betrayal, disappointment and disillusionment and hence minimize its need to create a protective establishment. If the group demands the generosity of its members, then it must adapt a generous attitude in return. In everyday speech such an attitude is referred to through phrases such as 'it takes all sorts' and 'live and let live'. It is a tolerant attitude permissive of diversity but one nevertheless difficult to bear, for the greater the intensity of one's own commitment the more it cries out to be requited.

Most importantly, however, the group must itself be capable of maintaining the dominance of its own depressive attitude. This means, despite its sense of vision and grandiosity, retaining the capacity to keep a sense of perspective and, hence, knowing that what might be created will not be perfect but could be good enough. This also means understanding that as the group objectifies itself and realizes its project, the revolutionaries will become a new establishment, that those who, for the time being, are part of the solution are at that very moment being dragged inexorably towards being part of the next problem. For the life of the group this is what we might call a critical realism, but one turned inwards upon its own process. The issue facing the group then is this: how is it possible to create an establishment which has more of the quality of being benign and less of the quality of being destructive? This is the issue to which we must now turn. But first a slight detour will be necessary.

THE FREEDOM OF OPPOSITION

As I have already hinted, the line of argument that I am developing is, I feel, different from that of other writers of the Left, such as Sartre (1976), Touraine (1981) and Polan (1984) who have also written with insight about the psychology of the group and the movement. Where I disagree with them is over their assumption that the creative group can only exist through the experience of a non-benign opposition. As Polan (1984, p. 184) puts it, 'The apocalyptic group depends upon the existence of an enemy – not a theoretical or ideological one, above all not a distant one, but one that is real in the sense that it is present and immediate as a threat.' Similarly, Touraine (1981, p. 81) poses three constitutive principles of a social movement: the principle of 'identity' (in whose name is one fighting?), the principle of 'totality' (on what grounds?) and the principle of 'opposition' (against whom?). The group, then, is a gamble. It acknowledges the threat and pledges itself to a dual struggle against a real enemy and its own paranoia. For Sartre, the gamble is itself the act of freedom; freedom is a moment, not a condition. Polan (1984, p. 189) puts it thus: 'Man has not entered the realm of freedom because no such objective kingdom of the free exists . . . Freedom exists only to the extent that it is constantly recreated by the commitment of each to the common project.'

The gamble is a heroic one, for even if it is successful in removing an existing social order it must eventually create a new establishment. And this is not to be simply explained away by the notion of betrayal, a notion based upon the splitting of the bad leaders from the good people. Rather, because 'an establishment' resides within each one of us, we become complicit in the creation of a new order, an order which promises to contain the conflicts between us, an order which is the recipient of a willing abandonment of freedom by the members of the group. As Polan (1984, p. 196) states, at some point after the revolutionary festival, the average individual retreats from constant participation to a necessary quietude, 'and the institution awaits'. Having achieved the work of transformation, 'the movement' becomes 'the new given', an inertial force beckoning the new social movements.

Sartre's vision of freedom is a tragic one. He asks us to commit ourselves to the pursuit of a moment in time, not because of what it might achieve but for its own sake: to enjoy the moment, for itself, despite the knowledge, not only of its inevitable passing, but of its transformation into the antithesis of freedom, the new order. The bleakness of this vision lies in the absence of any idea of 'progress', that the revolution might create an establishment which was more benign than the one that went before. For Polan, the nature of the new order is only pre-given to the extent that we abandon our freedom and responsibility:

Do we replace one set of frozen relations with another? Do we use our freedom to remain free, or do we use that freedom to decide to become, once again, unfree? . . . and so the gamble is not a once-and-for-all attempt at liberty, but the constant nature of man's negotiation of his relationship to the world and his fellows. (1984, p. 193)

For Polan, then, there is a way out from Sartre's recursive vision of order, movement, transformation and order. The exit lies in our collective willing-ness constantly to renew our commitment to freedom, to make of it an ethic, 'the ethic'. This is an attractive position, in many ways reminiscent of the Tavistock Group Relations tradition with its constant stress upon the ulti-mate responsibility of individuals for the actions they take or fail to take. However, there are some thoughts which spring to mind. For one thing, does such an ethic not take us too far in the direction of Schafer's (1976) action language; a direction that Ogden (1986) wisely cautions us against. Schafer is at pains to illustrate how our use of language is unconsciously designed to disavow our responsibility for what we think, feel or do. It is a reified language in which phantasmic forces are constructed and held responsible for our own behaviour: the woman who attributes her depress-ion to her 'nerves'; the colleague who attributes his isolation to 'the institution' for which he works; rivalrous community groups who attribute their inability to get along together to a 'meddling bureaucracy'. According to Schafer (1976, p. 154), through action-disclaiming language we uncon-sciously protest, 'Allow us our illusions of ignorance, passivity and help-lessness. We dare not acknowledge that we are masters in our own house.'

Now the problem with this argument is not that we don't constantly reify our worlds in this way; clearly we do, and equally clearly we do this partly because we are cowards and partly because, as I have mentioned elsewhere (Chapter 5), of the surplus objectivity demanded by the establishment of its subjects. But, and this is the point that Ogden makes so tellingly, we also disclaim responsibility because we were not responsible: we were not free agents at the time but vehicles through which psychosomatic and social forces found expression. To live the full life of freedom and agency would be equivalent to securing oneself permanently within the depressive posi-tion, whereas in reality, even where individual development has proceeded most smoothly, the non-psychotic element of the personality always re-mains a matter of 'more or less'. The idea of the individual constantly striving for freedom gives us a one-sided account of what it is to be human. It is not just 'the average individual' who must eventually seek quietude; we all must if we are not to die of emotional exhaustion. As Ogden (1986, p. 84) notes, 'Schafer's action language overstates the degree to which we are subjects and underestimates the degree to which the self forever remains an object.' The issue is not whether we should abandon our subjectivity or not, for it has to be relinquished if we are to live; rather, it is whether we can endeavour to become subjects for at least the major part of our lives. Those who would suggest that this statement lacks ambition would do well to ponder the degree of hegemony exercised by our internal and external establishments and the explosiveness of subjectivity once it has found a bit of elbow room within such systems. Once the genie is out of the bottle it will not rest until its work of transformation is complete.

Another point at which one might take issue with Polan is the way in which he implicitly ties freedom to the function of opposition. Is it true that only oppositional groups and dissidents can taste freedom? Can one be subversive only when moving against something? Can one not have a 'creative order' or a 'subversive establishment'? Why should those in opposition always be given the best cards to play?

The key issue for socialist and nationalist movements today is precisely this: we know how to act freely in opposition but we have not yet learned how to create in freedom. How does a creative and transformative group or movement retain its life-affirming properties one it has become the new order? And this is not just a question for the 'big revolution out there', it is of equal relevance to all micro-revolutionaries who seek to transform local institutions (communities, work organizations, local government, etc) into something better, whether in their role as managers, church leaders, community activists or whatever. How do we create a better establishment, one that delights in the flowering of its members' subjectivity rather than skulking in fear and hatred of such an eventuality? How, then, do we create institutions in our own image, true to our values, an establishment which nurtures its own opposition by being confident both in its own temporary authority and in its acknowledgement that, in the very moment of its creation, its time has already begun to pass?

Part of the answer must lie in the fault immanent within the principle of opposition itself. If a group or movement constitutes itself only or primarily through this means its moment of freedom can only be transitory and it will inevitably become its own antithesis. Oppositionalism indeed has been the curse of social movements for much of this century. How difficult it has been for the group to define itself in terms, not just of what it is against, but in terms of what it is for. It might be said that the recent struggle of the British miners was an exception. After all, was not their central slogan a preservative one: to preserve 'jobs and communities'? In part this was, of course, correct; it was an expression of the defensive struggle in which they found themselves. The problem was that they never managed to go properly on to the offensive, to put forward a clear alternative for their own future. What alternative was proposed to the management and organization of the National Coal Board, that unaccountable Morrisonian[7] bureaucracy? Is there no alternative between privatization and public bureaucracy? How were jobs and communities to be preserved? What alternative plan for energy (taking into account the environmental costs of existing coal-based forms of energy production) was put forward? Above all, what alternatives were generated to the existing patriarchal work-based structures of the National Union of Miners? When the union establishment was challenged by the transformative power of the miners' wives and the pit communities, it closed its doors. And this perhaps encapsulates the essential issue: the tendency for transformative movements to hold on to a profoundly split notion of change which projects the transformative impulse entirely on to the external environment whilst leaving its internal environment undisturbed. What Sartre and others perhaps failed to make explicit is that even during the moment of transformation an establishment lurks within the movement, an establishment which is unaware of itself, precisely because at that moment it embraces nearly the whole movement of 'people like us'. The question of 'creating in our own image' cannot therefore be left to the future but is a question which faces any group or movement in its here-and-now. Does the group itself, as an internal environment, constitute a benign force pushing towards a benign future or is it a deceit, a malignant body which destroys its own members' subjectivity in pursuit of an idealized future?

THE BENIGN ESTABLISHMENT

The question is one of ends and means. How does the group or movement, in the way it conducts itself and gives form to its internal life, give expression to the kind of vision that it has of the future? How in the present does it prefigure the possibilities it seeks to realize? Partly this is a question of leadership. As Ken Tarbuck notes, there are many who will accept the fact of rulers and ruled in society but refuse to accept the reality of leaders and led:

> In other words to be a ruler one must also be a leader, and even if one wants to abolish this condition one must start from this premise. However the style and content of the leadership for such a task becomes very different from that of leaders who wish to maintain the ruler/ruled relationship. There is a dialectical relationship here that has to be grasped, the leader who wishes to remain dominant will adopt very different methods from the one who prepares for his own supercession – in this respect there is a very clear and close relationship between means and ends. The led must be taken to the point where they become self-activating and the ruled self-ruling. (Tarbuck, 1977, p. 8)

One of the most disturbing characteristics of the Left today lies in the way in which it fails to develop its membership intellectually or personally. Ostensibly progressive organizations ignore their members' own needs; the 'needs of the struggle' are counterposed to the needs of the individual with monotonous regularity. For the majority, politics has become a most unpleasurable experience, inducing a number of splits within their lives and personalities. A split is maintained between 'work' and 'leisure': political activity is work; leisure is something to be taken 'outside politics'. There is also a split between ideas that are 'serious' and ideas that are 'unserious' (most of this book would be regarded as 'unserious'); a split between what is 'political' and what is 'personal', the minimum requirement being that one keep one's personal life out of politics (but not the opposite – how many families have been destroyed by the demands that one's partner's, usually the mate's, politics makes upon the others?). Finally, above all, there is a split between 'myself' and the movement or class: I am involved in politics in order to develop the confidence, understanding and strength of the class, not particularly to develop these qualities in myself. One might ask how the class can be developed through my efforts if I remain undeveloped: the answer lies in 'the party'. 'I may be weak, but my party is strong.' The party, then, assumes a reified existence; it is 'above' its membership. As Gramsci noted:

> If each of the individual members sees the collective organism as an entity external to himself, it is evident that this organism no longer in fact exists, it becomes a phantasm of the mind, a fetish.... What is astonishing and typical, is that fetishism of this kind occurs too in

'voluntary' organisms, not of a 'public' or State character, like parties and trade unions. (1977, p. 187)

There is also a crucial relationship between the needs of the individual and the problem of discipline. Discipline, a necessary condition for any real, rather than formal, association of labour, cannot be achieved through activity based upon duty.

As much as the individual may struggle to be 'a good party member' a part of his personality will be 'outside' that activity, a part of him will inevitably be drawn towards 'more enjoyable things', towards areas that he has been encouraged to believe are 'unserious' or 'personally based'. These 'other areas' may include anything from enjoying sex to breeding aquatic fish or taking part in a rock group. Clearly, sex, hobbies and music have nothing to do with politics. The activists, in their reified world, in their split existence, parallel exactly the condition of the worker alienated at the point of production. His work takes on a disembodied form; 'he is' somewhere else, in his phantasies and plans.

In such instances the third element of Marx's[8] list of conditions necessary for effective rational action will be absent; *alienated* activity, whether at the point of production or within a political organization, cannot be constantly faithful and deliberative (that is, attentive). It will be essentially undisciplined, defying even the corrective efforts of the supervisors.

Can you imagine a Labour Party or Socialist Workers' Party branch meeting at which the floor is given over for half an hour to members to talk about their passion for cycling, their interest in astronomy or their expertise in growing cacti? But this is ridiculous only if we think of politics as somehow removed from everyday life and the myriad enthusiasms in which people find a space for their creativity. It is the narrowness of our own political culture which constitutes such activities as 'escapism' rather than the bedrock of a fully human and transformative outlook.

There is a disturbing paradox within the Left today. Within the ranks of most of the political groups exist a large number of teachers and lecturers, all of whom are familiar with current educational theory. The vast majority of these persons will be able to present a vigorous defence of the more progressive aspects of this theory: the idea that a child cannot simply learn by the repetition of spellings, multiplications, etc.; that the child cannot learn simply by the accumulation of unrelated facts or simply by the appropriate   juxtaposition of rewards and punishments. They will be familiar with the notion that the infant and the child of primary school age primarily learn by experiment and discovery. They will be familiar with the notion that the young child (if allowed) interacts with the world in a creative fashion, has a desire to take in new experiences, extend its capabilities, answer unanswered questions. They should also be familiar with the idea that it becomes the task of 'education' to inhibit, if not destroy, this early creativeness. There is no place for it in society. Yet these same people, in the context of an organization where it becomes possible for these lost arts to be cultivated again, comply with a *modus operandi* that differs little in form from the established educational practice of our schools and, indeed, may sometimes in fact be worse.

Every infant is a scientist in her own right, knows the pleasure of new experiences and understandings; yet to activists today the notion that politics should be predicated on the notion of pleasure is quite unthinkable. Pleasure remains a dirty word.

Before leaving the issues of leaders and led, politics and pleasure, there is a final paradox that should be noted. For the establishment to prepare the grounds for its own supersession it must be willing to constitute itself as a tradition against which a new class or generation can pit itself. In other words, a benign establishment cannot afford to be too tolerant; it must be prepared to draw the line, otherwise it becomes so indistinct that it becomes impossible for constituent groups to define themselves against it and their development will be undermined. This is the point Rustin (1988) makes in his comparison of the Kleinian and object-relations tendencies within psychoanalysis. The tolerant and ecumenical climate of the latter group, Rustin suggests, has allowed it to absorb and assimilate a variety of theoretical developments but 'also to limit what might be thought a much-needed disturbance' (p. 137). Of the Kleinians, however, he notes:

> It can't be denied that dogmatism and the exercise of heavy-handed institutional authority have sometimes existed in the Kleinian school, with inhibiting effect. But on the other hand, the Kleinians' commitment to the pure essence of psychoanalysis, and to rigorous theory and method according to their lights, did bring about a second generation of innovative ideas. (p. 142)

A benign establishment, therefore, must not be afraid of becoming 'an authority', but it must be an authority that knows itself and in this sense has a capacity for reflexiveness. We might say that its authority should have an 'as if' quality about it. In other words, it should not lose the original quality of playfulness which was so necessary for its own empowerment. I am suddenly aware that in speaking of authority in this way we may have a generalized proposition about the exercise of benign authority in any context: in the family, in the office or in the classroom.

SPEAKING TRUTH TO POWER

The expression 'speaking truth to power' which, I believe, originated from the Quaker, William Penn, brings us finally up against the need for the creative group or movement to contain the capacity to keep questioning itself; to keep throwing the truth back at its own collective and internal establishment. The silencing effect of power is only too obvious in the external world; through such processes whole cultures have at times lost their voices.[9] But the group has its own power to silence; a power which comes from its own need to create a protective establishment.

Against this power the group must nurture its own collective capacity to challenge this establishment, its myths, its lies and its propaganda. This is equivalent to the group containing the function of self-analysis, the capacity to challenge 'the facts' which seem incontrovertible. It is the capacity to interrogate one's collective motives, get hold of them, place them on the table for examination and dissect them;[10] to be able to assume the position of the other, of the opponents, looking at oneself, at one's group. This group, which speaks of change, of liberation, of enlightenment; this group which, through its actions, seeks to lay bare the deceits of others, what for this group is unspeakable and therefore collectively unthinkable; what idea, or action, for this group, would be catastrophic?

Every group, even the most creative, will have its area of silence where its body is sensitive and should be touched upon only with care. It is the area where experience cannot be thought about and therefore must be thought about; it is the vicinity of the 'primary pain',[11] of what Puget (1988, p. 124) calls 'possible but intolerable knowledge'. In all situations there are some things which have to be said. The question is, does one love the group sufficiently to be an object of its hatred? For this is what is meant by the phrase 'to be cruel to be kind'.

The problem of means and ends brings us back to Bion and his undeveloped concept, the Work Group. It strikes me that terror plays a part in the life of all groups and not just those dominated by basic assumption activity. At every level of life the establishment is engaged in running its protection racket. If we live according to its bidding, it looks after us. If we challenge its hegemony it not only threatens to withdraw its 'privileges' but to send its agents round to visit. Ultimately the protection that is sought is protection from the phantasy of psychical death; in this case the death of the family, the group, the party or the institution to which we have given ourselves and through which we have found meaning. This returns us to Bion's dialectic of the container and the contained. As a container of meaning, the body of the group constitutes a prism through which reality is apprehended, but in the very process of constituting such perspective these social forms also entrap us and make the task of developing new forms a dangerous business. For what is contained is not just meaning but anxiety – in the last instance, terror of non-being. The problem of the creative group is to give protection without bondage and to provide support without enslavement. As I have put it, this boils down to the creation of a benign rather than a malignant establishment.

In the preceding sections I have tried to suggest that, if this is to occur, it is not enough for a group simply to be bound by a common purpose, even though this purpose may be no more than 'to make things better' (that is, be reparative in its intent). The purpose must be, in Weber's sense, 'substantive': one which seeks to integrate moral, technical and aesthetic considerations. The problem of the past has been the way in which groups have split off their liberatory intent from the means by which this was to be achieved. The alternative that I have posed is one in which the question of means, of technique, ceases to be simply a question of efficacy and becomes, instead, equivalent to the process by which one's intent is prefigured through the process of organizing for change itself. From this emerges the possibility, glimpsed by Gramsci, Touraine and others, of a new revolutionary aesthetic in which the group, through its capacity for play, its hedonism, its reflexivity and its capacity for self-analysis, endeavours to be a truly subjective body. Whilst I call such an aesthetic 'revolutionary', it should be clear by now that I do not intend to restrict this principle simply to formally recognized political activity. The 'carryings-on' of political parties are but a small element of the politics of life in which, as parents, professionals, trade unionists, managers, artists, volunteers, women, black, gay, community or church activists, we seek to create a better future, not on some far-off day but here and now.

NOTES

1 This argument was developed in more detail by Robinson (1984, pp. 182–5).

2 This line of argument also surfaces repeatedly within the Tavistock Group Relations tradition. See, for example, Turquet (1975).

3 Excellent summaries of Winnicott's work are provided by Davis and Wallbridge (1981) and Ogden (1986).

4 With hindsight, we now know that Arthur Scargill, the British miners' leader, was perfectly rational, indeed brilliantly perceptive, when he argued in the early 1980s that the Conservative Government planned to close down over half the operational pits in the UK; make redundant over 100,000 workers and then sell off what was left to the private sector. The problem was that almost everyone else in Britain thought he was crazy: even his staunchest allies thought he was a bit 'over the top'. As it turned out, even Scargill's analysis erred on the side of caution. Being correct doesn't win victories – socialism is rich in analysis, but when it comes to the politics of change much of this tradition has been tragically weak.

5 The Famous Five were the central characters in a series of books produced by the classic mid-twentieth-century writer of children's fiction, Enid Blyton.

6 'Objectification', the process by which an object is achieved through the interaction of the subject and her intention, the raw material and the means of production. See p. 16.

7 Herbert Morrison was the architect of the big British Public Corporation which emerged as a consequence of the nationalization programme of the post-war Attlee Government.

8 See pp. 19–20.

9 I have explored this effect of power in more detail in an earlier article (Hoggett, 1986).

10 Touraine (1981, pp. 166–72) develops a similar but more detailed argument in which he suggests that it is necessary for social movements to develop two levels of reflexivity. The first 'flexion' brings about a shift from the 'witness group' (one engaged directly in confrontation but without any self-awareness) to the 'image group' (in which the life of the group, its tensions, mythologies and psychodynamics can be considered as the mirror or transference of the wider movement of which it

is a part). The second 'flexion' transforms the 'image group' into the 'analyst group' (a group having the capacity to consider itself as its own object, in which the recognition of diversity can be used to enhance the group's intelligence and thus its capacity for imaginative struggle). Each 'flexion' strengthens the group's ability 'to conduct its own analysis, to adapt a distance to its own experience' (p. 170).

11 I first came across this idea at a paper given by Anton Obholzer at the first 'Psychoanalysis and the Public Sphere' conference in London in 1987. His choice of term was to some extent a deliberate device to contrast it to the concept of 'primary task' which has played such a central role within the Tavistock Group Relations tradition.

8

Beyond a Joke

So, what is there to say by way of conclusion? The power of the lie, the liar, and the one who wishes to be lied to. In the autumn of 1989, I watched as thousands fled from East to West, from the lie of the state and the party to the lie of the commodity. Organized terror may have one redeeming feature: it doesn't need to lie about itself too much. Consent, on the other hand, is a wonderful thing. How 'cultivated' we are in the West; such a degree of organization in our collective self-deception. But how do *we* lie, each one of us, in our everyday lives? By not putting 'two and two together': what we think with what we feel; what we do with what we say. Such kidology! Such an apparently inexhaustible capacity to kid ourselves that we are 'taking a stand' when all the time we are merely settling accounts with 'the powers that be'. And then there are those who preach because they cannot practise, for whom change is always externalized, other, not me, out there. Emotional cripples, cold and hateful, mirroring the terror they seek to challenge.

In this book I have tried to give psychoanalytic pessimism its leash; to say, 'how difficult life is', especially for those who would take a stand. But I have done this not in order to encourage despair, for I doubt whether I have the internal capacity to assume such an attitude. Anger I have plenty enough, and hatred too; but I have also hope: the hope that comes when acquaintances confound the mean expectations I have of them; the hope that comes when I see my own children stay with difficult or painful experiences and grow visibly as individuals; the hope that comes when groups, against all odds, stand up to terror and fight for justice – in the former GDR, in South Korea, in El Salvador, in Brazil and, of course, here in Britain; even here, groups still fight on.

But, of course, how else could things be? For if we are liars we are also truth-seekers. We have it in us, therefore, to create a world where truthfulness is not attacked but sustained and nourished, and where power is used to empower rather than to oppress.

Psychoanalysis also shows us the power of truth; the way in which it draws us to it, through a ceaseless process of learning, unlearning and relearning. A constant process, from the intra-uterine environment onwards, of pushing at the boundaries of things, of testing the given. And, at the highest level, the capacity to test and question the boundaries of our own certainties, that is, to be reflexive towards our own experience. Nothing is ever quite what it seems: that reflexive moment, in which one's own experience, at that very instant in time, becomes an object of scrutiny; that capacity to hold on to a tiny suspicion, a little murmur of disturbance, to clear a space from which it may emerge through all the hubbub of the internal world. You might call it simple honesty, but how hard one's own internal establishment fights against it, let alone the establishment within the group.

In this book I have not just tried to celebrate an attitude towards life which might be called subversive. For in one sense we, on the Left, have always had it easy, because we have rarely held power we know only how to criticize those with power. Surely the supreme art is to be a subversive 'in power'.

A powerful subversive? Gorbachev? Surely that's naive! As a man of the Left I should have realized what he was up to. He was a modernizer; no more, no less.

And Walesa and Havel too? Of course!

How comforting are our categories! Dare we go beyond them. Just to entertain the possibility that . . . that there might be more here than meets the eye. Heaven forbid, man, have you gone soft! No, but I fear my categories have.

Ah! I remember that lovely phrase now: 'Your problem, sir, is that you suffer from a hardening of the categories.' An old joke, I know, but a good one nevertheless!

Bibliography

Place of publication is London unless otherwise specified.

Adorno, T.W., Brunswick, E., Levinson, D.J. and Nevitt Sandford, R. (1950) *The Authoritarian Personality*. New York: Harper & Row.

Alford, R. (1975) *Health Care Politics: Ideological and Interest Group Barriers to Reform*. Chicago: University of Chicago Press.

Anderson, P. (1976) 'The antimonies of Antonio Gramsci', *New Left Review* 100: 5–78.

Anzieu, D. (1984) *The Group and the Unconscious*. Routledge & Kegan Paul.

Bacharach, S.B. and Lawler, E.J. (1980) *Power and Politics in Organizations*. San Francisco: Josey-Bass.

Balint, M. (1959) *Thrills and Regressions*. Hogarth.

—— (1979) *The Basic Fault*. Tavistock.

Baranger, M., Baranger, W. and Mon, J.M. (1988) 'The infantile psychic trauma from us to Freud: pure trauma, retroactivity and reconstructions', *Int. J. Pyscho-Anal*. 69: 113–28.

Baron, P.A. and Sweezey, P.M. (1966) *Monopoly Capital*. Harmondsworth: Penguin.

Bateson, G. (1973) *Steps to an Ecology of Mind*. Paladin.

Baudrillard, J. (1983) 'The ecstasy of communication', in H. Foster, ed. *The Anti-Aesthetic: Essays in Postmodern Culture*. Port Townsend, WA: Bay Press, pp. 126–34.

Benjamin, J. (1978) 'Authority and the family revisited: or, a world without fathers?', *New German Critique* 13: 35–57.

Benson, K. (1982) 'A framework for policy analysis', in D. Rogers and D. Whetter, eds *Interorganizational Coordination*. Ames, Iowa: Iowa State University Press, pp. 137–75.

Bercherie, P. (1986) 'The quadrifocal oculary: the epistemology of the Freudian heritage', *Economy and Society* 15(1): 23–70.

Bick, E. (1968) 'Experience of the skin in early object relations', *Int. J. Psycho-Anal*. 49: 484–6.

—— (1986) 'Further considerations on the function of the skin in early object relations: findings from infant observation integrated into child and adult analysis', *Br. J. Psychoth*. 2(4): 292–9.

Bion, W. (1957a) 'On arrogance', *Int. J. Psycho-Anal.* 144; reprinted in *Second Thoughts: Selected Papers on Psycho-Analysis.* New York: Jason Aronson, 1976, pp. 86–92.

—— (1957b) 'Differentiation of the psychotic from the non-psychotic personalities', *Int. J. Psycho-Anal.* 38: 266–75.

—— (1961) 'Group dynamics', in *Experience in Groups.* Tavistock, pp. 141–91.

—— (1962) *Learning from Experience.* Heinemann.

—— (1970) *Attention and Interpretation.* Tavistock.

—— (1987) *The Long Weekend.* Free Association Books.

Brown, D. (1985) 'Bion and Foulkes: basic assumptions and beyond', in M. Pines, ed. *Bion and Group Psychotherapy.* Routledge & Kegan Paul, pp. 192–219.

Chasseguet-Smirgel, J. (1985a) *Creativity and Perversion.* Free Association Books.

—— (1985b) *The Ego Ideal: A Psychoanalytic Essay on the Malady of the Ideal.* Free Association Books.

Chiesa, M. (1986) 'The Milan systemic approach to family therapy: an overview', *Free Associations* 5: 28–47.

Clegg, S. (1981) 'Organization and Control', *Administrative Science Quarterly* 26: 545–62.

Collier, A. (1977) *R.D. Laing: The Philosophy and Politics of Psychotherapy.* Brighton: Harvester.

Colletti, L. (1972) *From Rousseau to Lenin.* New Left Books.

Cooper, R. and Burrell, G. (1988) 'Modernism, postmodernism and organizational analysis: an introduction', *Organizational Studies* 9(1): 91–112.

D'Amico, R. (1986) 'Going relativist', *Telos* 67: 135–45.

Davis, M. and Wallbridge, D. (1981) *Boundary and Space: An Introduction to the Work of D.W. Winnicott.* Karnac.

Eagleton, T. (1985) 'Capitalism, modernism and postmodernism', *New Left Review* 152: 60–73.

Ehrenreich, J., ed. (1978) *The Cultural Crisis of Modern Medicine.* Monthly Review Press.

Etzioni, A. (1961) *A Comparative Analysis of Complex Organizations.* Glencoe, IL : Free Press.

Fanon, F. (1967) *Black Skin, White Masks.* New York: Grove Press.

Fayol, H. (1916) Administration industrielle et générale, Bulletin de la Societé de l'Industrie Minérale. English translation, *General and Industrial Management*, Pitman, 1971.

Freud, S. (1896) 'The aetiology of hysteria', in James Strachey, ed. *The Standard Edition of the Complete Psychological Works of Sigmund Freud*, 24 vols. Hogarth, 1953–73. vol. 3, pp. 189–221.

—— (1905) *Three Essays on Sexuality. S.E.* 7, pp. 125–245.

—— (1911) 'Psycho-analytic notes on an autobiographical account of a case of paranoia'. *S.E.* 12, pp. 9–79.

—— (1915a) 'Instincts and their vicissitudes'. *S.E.* 14, pp. 109–40.

—— (1915b) 'The unconscious'. *S.E.* 14, pp. 159–216.

—— (1917a) 'A metapsychological supplement to the theory of dreams'. *S.E.* 14, pp. 222–35.

—— (1917b) 'Mourning and melancholia'. *S.E.* 14, pp. 237–58.

—— (1920) *Beyond the Pleasure Principle. S.E.* 18, pp. 3–64.

—— (1921) *Group Psychology and the Analysis of the Ego. S.E.* 18, pp. 67–143.

—— (1923) *The Ego and the Id. S.E.* 19, pp. 3–66.

—— (1925) 'On negation'. *S.E.* 19, pp. 235–9.

Giddens, A. (1979) *Central Problems in Social Theory*. Berkeley, CA: University of California Press.

Gosling, R. (1979) 'Another source of conservatism in groups', in W.G. Lawrence, ed. *Exploring Individual and Organizational Boundaries*. John Wiley, pp. 77–86.

Gramsci, A. (1977) *The Prison Notebooks*. Lawrence & Wishart.

Grotstein, J. (1985) *Splitting and Projective Identification*. New York: Jason Aronson.

Habermas, J. (1986) *The Theory of Communicative Action*. Cambridge: Polity.

Heimann, P. (1952) 'Certain functions of introjection and projection in early infancy', in M. Klein, P. Heimann, S. Isaacs and J. Rivière, eds *Developments in Psycho-Analysis*. Hogarth, pp. 122–68.

Hinshelwood, R.D. (1989) 'Social possession of identity', in B. Richards, ed. *Crises of the Self*. Free Association Books, pp. 75–83.

Hoggett, P. (1986) 'Aspects of longing', *Free Associations* 4: 120–38.

—— (1988) 'Try a little tenderness', *Chartist* 121: 12–14.

Hoggett, P. and Lousada, J. (1985) 'Therapeutic intervention in working-class communities', *Free Associations* 1: 125–52.

Hoggett, P. and McGill, I. (1988) 'Labourism: ends and means,' *Critical Social Policy* 23: 23–33.

Jameson, F. (1983) 'Postmodernism and the consumer society', in H. Foster, ed. *The Anti-Aesthetic: Essays on Postmodern Culture*. Port Townsend, WA: Bay Press, pp. 111–25.

Jaques, E. (1951) *The Changing Culture of a Factory*. Routledge & Kegan Paul.

Johnson, T. (1972) *Professions and Power*. Macmillan.

Jones, E. (1927) 'Early development of female sexuality', in *Papers on Psycho-Analysis*, 5th edn. Baillière, Tindall & Cox, 1950, pp. 438–45, and *Int. J. Psycho-Anal.* 8: 459–72.

Khan, R. Masud (1974) *The Privacy of the Self.* Hogarth.

Klein, M. (1930) 'The importance of symbol-formation in the development of the ego', *Int. J. Psycho-Anal.* 11: 24–39.

—— (1957) 'Envy and gratitude', in *Envy and Gratitude and Other Works 1946–1963*. Hogarth, pp. 176–235.

Klein, S. (1980) 'Autistic phenomena in neurotic patients', *Int. J. Psycho-Anal.* 61: 395–402.

Kovel, J. (1983) *Against the State of Nuclear Terror*. Pan.

Kuhn, T. (1970) *The Structure of Scientific Revolutions*. Chicago, IL: University of Chicago Press.

Lacy, S. (1982) *The Wire*, No. 1.

Laplanche, J. and Pontalis, J.-B. (1973) *The Language of Psychoanalysis*. Tavistock.

Lasch, C. (1978) *The Culture of Narcissism* New York: Norton.

—— (1985) *The Minimal Self: Psychic Survival in Troubled Times*. Pan.

Lenin, V. (1961) *Collected Works*, vol. 38. Lawrence & Wishart.

Levi, P. (1986) *The Periodic Table*. Abacus.

—— (1987) *If This Is a Man*. Harmondsworth: Penguin.

Lewin, K. (1948) *Resolving Social Conflicts*. New York: Harper & Row.

Liebman, M. (1975) *Leninism under Lenin*. Cape.

Lukács, G. (1971) *History and Class Consciousness*. Merlin.

Lyotard, J.-F. (1984) *The Postmodern Condition*. Minneapolis, MN: University of Minnesota Press.

Marcuse, H. (1964) *One-Dimensional Man: Studies in the Ideology of Advanced Industrial Society*. Routledge & Kegan Paul.

Marx, K. (1844) *Economic and Philosophical Manuscripts*. Lawrence & Wishart.

——— (1857/8) *Grundrisse.* Harmondsworth: Penguin, 1973.

——— (1876) *Capital,* vol. 1, Lawrence & Wishart, 1970.

Masuch, M. (1985) 'Vicious circles in organizations', *Administrative Science Quarterly.* 30: 14–33.

Meltzer, D. (1978) *The Kleinian Development Part III: The Clinical Significance of the Work of W.E. Bion.* Perthshire: Clunie.

Meltzer, D., Bremmer, J., Hoxter, S., Weddell, D. and Wittenberg, I. (1975) *Explorations in Autism,* Perthshire: Clunie.

Meltzer, D. (1986) *Studies in Extended Metapsychology: Clinical Applications of Bion's Ideas.* The Roland Harris Educational Trust.

Menzies, I. (1959) The functioning of social systems as a defence against anxiety', *Human Relations* 13(2): 95–121.

Merton, R. (1957) 'Bureaucratic structure and personality', in *Social Theory and Social Structure.* Glencoe, IL: Free Press.

Miliband, R. (1985) 'The new revisionism in Britain', *New Left Review* 150: 5–26.

Miller, A. (1988) *The Drama of Being a Child.* Virago.

Miller, E.J. (1977) 'Organizational development and industrial democracy: a current case-study', in C. Cooper, ed. *Organizational Development in the UK and US: A Joint Evaluation.* Macmillan.

——— (1979) 'Open systems revisited: a proposition about development and change', in W.G. Lawrence *Exploring Individual and Organizational Boundaries.* John Wiley, pp. 217–33.

Miller, H. (1966) *Sexus.* Panther.

Milner, M. (1955) 'The role of illusion in symbol formation', in M. Klein, P. Heimann and R. Money-Kyrle, eds *New Directions in Psycho-Analysis.* Tavistock, pp. 82–108.

Morris Suzuki, T. (1984) 'Robots and capitalism', *New Left Review,* 147: 109–21.

——— (1986) 'Capitalism in the computer age', *New Left Review* 160: 81–91.

Moss Kanter, R. (1985) *The Change Masters: Corporate Entrepreneurs at Work.* Counterpoint, Unwin Paperbacks.

Nuttall, J. (1968) *Bomb Culture.* Paladin.

Offe, C. (1984) *Contradictions of the Welfare State.* Hutchinson.

Ogden, T. (1986) *The Matrix of the Mind.* New York: Jason Aronson.

Peres, C. (1983) 'Structural change and the assimilation of new technologies in the economic and social system', *Futures* 15: 357–75.

Peters, T. and Waterman, R. (1982) *In Search of Excellence: Lessons from America's Best-Run Companies*. Harper & Row.

Polan, A.J. (1984) *Lenin and the End of Politics*. Methuen.

Poster, M. (1978) *Critical Theory of the Family*. Pluto.

Puget, J. (1988) 'Social violence and psychoanalysis in Argentina: the unthinkable and the unthought', *Free Associations* 13: 84–140.

Reicher, S. and Potter, J. (1985) 'Psychological theory as intergroup perspective: a comparative analysis of "scientific" and "lay" accounts of crowd behaviour', *Human Relations* 38(2): 167–89.

Relph, E. (1976) *Place and Placelessness*. Pion.

Rice, A.K. (1976) 'Individual, group and intergroup process', In E. Miller ed. *Task and Organization*. John Wiley.

Robinson, S. (1984) 'The parent to the child', in B. Richards, ed. *Capitalism and Infancy*. Free Association Books, pp. 167–206.

Rodrigue, E. (1956) 'Notes on symbolism', *Int. J. Psycho-Anal.* 37: 147–58.

Rustin, M. (1988) 'Shifting paradigms in psychoanalysis since the 1940s', *History Workshop Journal* 26: 133–42.

Sargent, P. (1988) 'Leisure and retailing: an exciting synergy', *Leisure Management* 8(9): 36–40.

Sartre, J.P. (1976) *Critique of Dialectical Reason*. New Left Books.

Schafer, R. (1976) *A New Language for Psychoanalysis*. New Haven, CT: Yale University Press.

Schatzman, M. (1976) *Soul Murder*. Harmondsworth: Penguin.

Schmidt, A. (1971) *Marx's Conception of Nature*. New Left Books.

Schneider, M. (1975) *Neurosis and Civilization*. New York: Seabury Press.

Searles, H. (1960) *Nonhuman Environment in Normal Development and in Schizophrenia*. New York: International Universities Press.

Segal, H. (1986) 'Notes on symbol formation', in *The Work of Hanna Segal*. Free Association Books, pp. 49–65.

Shields, R. (1989) 'Social spatialization and the built environment: the West Edmonton Mall', *Environment & Planning D: Society & Space* 7: 147–64.

Silverman, H. (1988) 'Retailing trends', *Leisure Management* 8(12): 44–6.

Sloterdijk, P. (1984) 'Cynicism – the twilight of false consciousness', *New German Critique* 33: 190–206.

Spengler, O. (1926) *The Decline of the West*, vol. 1. Allen & Unwin.

Steiner, J. (1985) 'Turning a blind eye: psychotic states and the cover-up for Oedipus', *Int. Rev. Psycho-Anal.* 12(2): 161–72.

Stevens, T. (1988) 'The Baltimore story', *Leisure Management* 8(11): 54–61.

Stewart, R. (1982) *Choices for the Manager: A Guide to Managerial Work and Behaviour.* McGraw-Hill.

Szekacs, J. (1985) 'Impaired spatial structures', *Int. J. Psycho-Anal.* 66: 193–9.

Tarbuck, K. (1977) 'Marxism, method and revolution', *Intervention* 1:1 –20.

Thompson, E.P. (1970) 'Writing by candlelight', *New Society,* 24 December 1970.

Touraine, A. (1981) *The Voice and the Eye: An Analysis of Social Movements.* Cambridge: Cambridge University Press.

Trotsky, L. (1921) 'Report on "the balance sheet" of the Third Congress of the Communist International', in L. Trotsky (1972) *The First Five Years of the Communist International,* vol. 1. Monad Press, pp. 297–312.

—— (1923) 'The curve of capitalist development', reprinted in *Fourth International,* May 1941, pp. 35–41.

Turquet, P. (1975) 'Threats to identity in the large group', in L. Kreeger ed. *The Large Group: Dynamics and Therapy.* Constable.

Tustin, F. (1986) *Austistic Barriers in Neurotic Patients.* Karnac.

Waddell, M. (1989) 'Living in two worlds: psychodynamic theory and social work practice', *Free Associations* 15: 11–35.

Watzlawick, P., Beavin, J. and Jackson, D. (1968) *Pragmatics of Human Communication.* Faber.

Weber, M. (1978) *Economy and Society* vol.1, G. Roth and C. Wittik, eds. Berkeley, CA: University of California Press.

Weick, K. (1976) 'Educational organizations as loosely coupled systems', *Administrative Science Quarterly* 21: 1–19.

Wilmott, H. (1986) 'Unconscious sources of motivation in the theory of the subject', *Journal for the Theory of Social Behaviour* 16: 106–19.

Winnicott, D.W. (1949) 'Mind and its relation to the psyche-soma', in Winnicott (1975), pp. 234–54.

—— (1950) 'Aggression in relation to emotional development,' in Winnicott (1975), pp. 204–18.

—— (1951) 'Transitional objects and transitional phenomena', in Winnicott (1975), pp. 229–42.

—— (1952) 'Psychoses and child care', in Winnicott (1975), pp. 219–28.

—— (1958) 'The capacity to be alone', in Winnicott (1976), pp. 29–36.

—— (1974) *Playing and Reality.* Harmondsworth: Penguin.

—— (1975) *Through Paediatrics to Psycho-Analysis.* Hogarth.

—— (1976) *The Maturational Processes and the Facilitating Environment*. Hogarth.

Wright, P. (1987) *Spycatcher: The Candid Autobiography of a Senior Intelligence Officer*. New York: Viking.

INDEX

This first edition of *Partisans in an Uncertain World:*
The Psychoanalysis of Engagement
was finished in February 1992.

The book was commissioned and edited by Robert M. Young,
designed by Wendy Millichap,
indexed by Linda English
and produced by Ann Scott
for Free Association Books.